A World of Wellbeing

Deirdre Murphy · Jim Ryan

The Educational Company of Ireland

First published 2018
The Educational Company of Ireland
Ballymount Road
Walkinstown
Dublin 12
www.edco.ie

A member of the Smurfit Kappa Group plc

ISBN 978-1-84536-776-3

Editors: Kristin Jensen, Dog's-ear
Design: Design Image
Layout: Design Image, Carole Lynch
Illustrator: Global Blended Learning
Proofreaders: Claire Reynolds, Dog's-ear
Cover Design: Design Image
Cover Photography: iStock/serkorkin; iStock/Trifonov_Evgeniy

The paper used in this book comes from Managed Forests in Northern Europe For every tree felled, at least one new tree is planted

Acknowledgements

We would like to express our thanks to our families for their unwavering encouragement and support during the writing process. We would particularly like to thank Kristin Jensen, Aoife Walsh, Niamh Parkinson, Emer Ryan and all the staff at Edco for their advice and guidance in bringing *A World of Wellbeing* to fruition.

While every care has been taken to trace and acknowledge copyright, the publishers tender their apologies for any accidental infringement where copyright has proved untraceable. They would be pleased to come to a suitable arrangement with the rightful owner in each case.

Copyright acknowledgements

Page 30, 'Fatima's Story', www.sendmyfriend.org. Used by permission; Page 49, Angelique Chrisafis, 'French law forbids food waste by supermarkets', The Guardian, 4 February 2016; Page 79, Gabriel Samuels, 'Muslim woman told to remove hijab by police on French beach before being racially abused', The Independent, 24 August 2016; Page 91; Pastor Martin Niemöller, 'First They Came'; Page 114, 'Cocoa Farmers and Workers', www.fairtrade.org.uk. Used by permission; Page 133, 'Now you see us: The human stories behind poverty in Ireland', www.communityplatform.ie; Page 135, Deborah Kyvrikosaios, 'Poverty-stricken Greek town hits new low', Reuters, 30 March 2012; Page 140, 'Brazil to write off $900m of African debt', www.aljazeera.com, 27 May 2013.

Web references in this book are intended as a guide for teachers. At the time of going to press, all web addresses were active and contained information relevant to the topics in this book. However, The Educational Company of Ireland and the authors do not accept responsibility for the views or information contained on these websites. Content and addresses may change beyond our control and pupils should be supervised when investigating websites.

05M23

Contents

Introduction

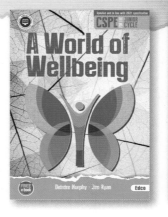
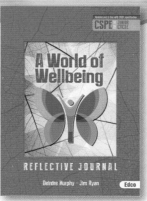

Welcome to *A World of Wellbeing!*

As you begin your journey in secondary school, you have probably become aware that this is a time of great change for you. You are a member of a new school community, with new classmates and teachers. You are also being introduced to new subjects. One such subject is Civic, Social and Political Education (CSPE). CSPE is a short course that belongs to an area of learning called Wellbeing.

A World of Wellbeing is a teaching and learning package that will support your learning as you engage with the CSPE short course. The package consists of:

🌐 *A World of Wellbeing* textbook

🌐 *A World of Wellbeing* reflective journal

🌐 *A World of Wellbeing* digital resources.

CSPE and Wellbeing

CSPE belongs to a new area of learning called Wellbeing. Wellbeing is about feeling well mentally, physically, emotionally and socially. When we have a strong sense of wellbeing, we can cope with the challenges presented by everyday life, live purposeful lives and have a sense of belonging to the wider community.

Through your study of CSPE, you will explore how your wellbeing is connected to the wellbeing of others in your community, the state and the wider world. You will learn about the importance of taking responsibility for your own wellbeing and the wellbeing of others. Happy and healthy citizens can create a World of Wellbeing.

MY WELLBEING + THE WELLBEING OF OTHERS
+ WELL COMMUNITIES + A WELL SOCIETY

= A WORLD OF WELLBEING

Animation Wellbeing Indicators Explained (Overview)

What is CSPE?

CSPE is a course in citizenship that will help you to develop the knowledge, skills and attitudes to participate actively in and make a positive contribution to democratic society.

What do the initials CSPE mean?

C – Civic	This refers to the idea of citizenship. As a citizen, you are entitled to certain rights. You also have responsibilities not only to yourself, but to others, your community and the wider world.
S – Social	This is about your relationship to society and the communities to which you belong.
P – Political	This refers to governments and the role that the government plays in shaping the lives of citizens.
E – Education	This refers to the knowledge, attitudes and skills that you will develop through your study of CSPE.

CSPE explores the idea of citizenship. Being a citizen involves belonging to a community. As a citizen, it is important that you have a sense of belonging or 'connectedness' to the many communities you belong to: your family, school, the local community, Ireland, the European Union and the wider world. You will learn about social, economic and political structures and how they can impact on individuals, communities and society at large.

Throughout your study of CSPE, you will have opportunities to consider ways in which you can get involved with your community and make a positive difference to the lives of others. For example, in Chapter 1 you will be introduced to the idea of active citizenship and how active citizens can contribute positively to the life of their communities.

As a citizen, you need to be aware of your rights and how these play a role in protecting your human dignity and the dignity of others. You will learn that with rights come responsibilities.

We need to take responsibility for our planet. You will examine the importance of living sustainably in order to protect our environment and natural resources for future generations.

You will also learn the importance of participating in a democratic society. This involves using your voice, getting involved in decision-making and playing a role in shaping the world around you.

How is the CSPE short course structured?

The CSPE short course is built on three strands of learning:

🌐 Strand 1: Rights and responsibilities

🌐 Strand 2: Global citizenship

🌐 Strand 3: Exploring democracy.

In this textbook, each strand is divided into themes called **units**.

Strand 1: Rights and responsibilities

Unit 1: Human dignity: The basis for human rights

Human dignity is the basis for human rights. An individual can live their life with dignity if their needs are met, their rights are respected and they are treated equally and fairly by others. In this unit, you will learn about your rights and responsibilities as a member of a community. Sometimes individuals or groups suffer a loss of human dignity. You will explore some situations where human dignity is not respected.

Unit 2: Human rights instruments

In this unit you will learn about the history of human rights and explore key human rights instruments (documents) that seek to promote and protect human rights. You will be introduced to individuals and organisations that have played an important role in protecting and promoting human rights. You will also understand the importance of taking responsibility to protect your human rights and those of others.

Strand 2: Global citizenship

Unit 3: Sustainability

Sustainability means meeting our present-day needs without endangering the ability of future generations to meet their own needs. In this unit you will learn about the importance of living sustainably. You will explore the concept of sustainable development and the ways in which we can practise sustainable living. Living sustainably involves caring for our planet and ensuring that the environment and our natural resources can be enjoyed by future generations.

Unit 4: Local and global development

Development involves change. Development can be positive or negative. There are many developments taking place in the world around you at both local and global levels. Development is influenced by both individuals and institutions.

Unit 5: Effecting global change

The world is in a constant state of change. Much of this change is caused by human activity. Change can have many consequences. Active citizens ensure that such changes are sustainable and positive.

Strand 3: Exploring democracy

Unit 6: The meaning of democracy

In this unit you will explore the concept of democracy and gain an understanding of how democracy works. You will examine how democracies interact with their citizens. You will explore some national and European democratic institutions.

Unit 7: The law and the citizen

Rules and laws are important in society. In this unit you will examine how laws are made and enforced and how they can impact on your everyday life. You will also explore the ways in which individuals and groups can change the law.

Unit 8: The role of the media in a democracy

The media plays an important role in a democratic society. In this unit you will explore the different forms of media. You will examine the importance of digital media and how it plays an increasingly important role in society today.

Activities

A World of Wellbeing has a range of activities that not only support your learning, but also provide opportunities for you to become actively involved in the learning process.

Connect and communicate

This feature encourages you to connect and communicate with an individual, group or organisation to find out more information about a topic or theme that is central to CSPE.

Create a video

These activities encourage you to engage with digital media to create a video or short film.

Debate

Debates enable you to voice your opinion and views on various issues. These activities encourage you to defend your viewpoint, engage in critical thinking and view situations from different perspectives.

Digital

The digital icon points you towards a wide variety of digital resources, such as animations, video clips and links to websites that can support your learning of CSPE. See page xiv for more details.

Group activity

Group activities provide opportunities to work with a small group to discuss an issue, complete a task, problem-solve or make decisions.

Imagine!

These activities promote creativity and require you to imagine situations or explore different perspectives on an issue.

Individual activity

These activities provide opportunities to think and work independently.

Questions

These activities require you to answer questions about a particular stimulus. They also help you to evaluate your learning.

Research

Research activities will help you to find out more about an issue, theme or topic. Research can be undertaken using books, magazines, newspapers, video clips, the internet or other media. Research can be undertaken independently, with a partner or as part of a group.

Role play

These activities require you to assume a role or identity in order to explore a situation or topic.

Take action!

These activities encourage you to practise active citizenship by taking action on an issue or topic. They also provide an opportunity to make a positive difference to your life and the lives of others, your community, the state or the wider world. You don't have to undertake all the 'take action' activities in this textbook. These activities can act as suggestions for future citizenship actions.

Think, pair and share

'Think, pair and share' activities combine working independently and working with a partner to complete a task, answer a question or problem-solve. These activities provide opportunities for both independent thinking and working with others.

Other textbook features

Learning outcomes:
This is what you should know, understand or be able to do by the end of the chapter.

Key words: Important words or terms that you should come to understand as a result of your learning in each chapter.

Key skills you will use in this chapter: These are the key skills you will use when undertaking the activities in the textbook and reflective journal.

Wellbeing indicators: These are the areas of Wellbeing that are important to your learning in each chapter.

Wellbeing indicators

These are questions you can ask about your wellbeing as you work through the CSPE short course. All of the Wellbeing indicators except Active are relevant to the CSPE short course.

Active

🌐 Am I a confident and skilled participant in physical activity?

🌐 How physically active am I?

Responsible

🌐 Do I take action to protect and promote my wellbeing and that of others?

🌐 Do I make healthy eating choices?

🌐 Do I know where my safety is at risk and do I make the right choices?

Connected

🌐 Do I feel connected to my school, my friends, my community and the wider world?

🌐 Do I appreciate that my actions and interactions impact on my own wellbeing and that of others, both in local and global contexts?

Resilient

🌐 Do I believe that I have the coping skills to deal with life's challenges?

🌐 Do I know where I can go for help?

🌐 Do I believe that with effort I can achieve?

Respected

🌐 Do I feel that I am listened to and valued?

🌐 Do I have positive relationships with my friends, my peers and my teachers?

🌐 Do I show care and respect for others?

Aware

🌐 Am I aware of my thoughts, feelings and behaviours and can I make sense of them?

🌐 Am I aware of what my personal values are and do I think through my decisions?

🌐 Do I understand what helps me to learn and how I can improve?

Taking action

Taking action is at the heart of the CSPE short course. You are required to undertake at least three **citizenship actions** as part of your learning across the three strands of the CSPE course. Undertaking citizenship actions enables you to practise active citizenship and take action on issues that you are interested in or feel strongly about.

Throughout your study of CSPE, you will be given opportunities to consider the ways in which you can make a positive difference to your community or the wider world. Taking action means turning these ideas into reality.

You can undertake a citizenship action as part of your class, as part of a group or as an individual. If you decide to take action as part of the class or as a group, it is important that everyone has a role to play in the planning and execution of the action.

Here are some examples of actions you can undertake:

🌐 Fundraising for an organisation

🌐 Organising a campaign

🌐 Conducting a survey

🌐 Inviting a guest speaker to talk to your class

🌐 Producing an information leaflet or booklet

🌐 Running a mock election

🌐 Investigating an issue

🌐 Visiting an organisation or institution

🌐 Raising awareness about an issue

🌐 Lobbying a public representative

🌐 Making a presentation

🌐 Promoting sustainable living through activities that protect our environment.

You will create a **Citizen Action Record** for **one** of these actions as part of your **classroom-based assessment (CBA)**. This should take place in Second or Third Year. Your Citizenship Action Record should show how you have actively engaged in an issue or topic of interest. You will describe the action undertaken and reflect on the whole process.

▶ **Animation** Steps to Action

Further information on undertaking and planning actions can be found in Chapter 35 at the end of this book.

And finally...

As a student of CSPE, you should be aware of what is going on in the world around you. It is important, therefore, that you keep track of events happening in your community, Ireland and the wider world. Being informed ensures that you can make connections between local and global events and your learning in CSPE. Newspapers, magazines, television and the radio are important sources of news and information. Don't forget about the digital media! This is a useful platform to access and share information. Social media platforms like Facebook and Twitter and search engines like Google can also be valuable sources of information.

Get informed, take action and help to create a World of Wellbeing!

Digital resources

The digital resources in *A World of Wellbeing* support the Junior Cycle's emphasis on the use of modern technology in the classroom and are designed to cater for different learning styles.

Teachers and students can access the *A World of Wellbeing* interactive e-book at **www.edcolearning.ie**, plus a bank of free digital resources, including animations and PowerPoint presentations, topic-based videos and useful weblinks.

Animations and PowerPoint presentations

Note: Click on the icons on this page in your e-book to access the animations and PowerPoints.

 Wellbeing Indicators Explained (Overview)

 Key Skill: Staying Well

 Wellbeing Indicator: Responsible

 Key Skill: Communicating

 Wellbeing Indicator: Connected

 Key Skill: Being Creative

 Wellbeing Indicator: Resilient

 Key Skill: Working with Others

 Wellbeing Indicator: Respected

 Key Skill: Managing Information and Thinking

 Wellbeing Indicator: Aware

 Steps to Action

 Key Skills Explained (Overview)

 Steps to Action

 Key Skill: Managing Myself

 Citizenship Action Record and Classroom-Based Assessment

 Topic-based videos

A range of informative and insightful topic-based videos is available to students and teachers. Links to these videos are embedded at the relevant points throughout the *A World of Wellbeing* e-book. Please note that the Amnesty International video is flagged as 'Teacher only', as the topic is sensitive, and viewing with the guidance of your teacher is advised.

Weblinks documents

A list of useful weblinks and resources is provided for each strand of this book, as well as an extra set of helpful resources for the Citizenship Action Record. These can be accessed via both the teacher and student e-book.

STRAND 1

RIGHTS AND RESPONSIBILITIES

Universal Declaration of Human Rights

In this strand you will learn about the importance of human rights and social responsibilities and how they can promote human dignity.

Unit 1   HUMAN DIGNITY: THE BASIS FOR HUMAN RIGHTS

Human dignity is the basis for human rights. We all have a responsibility to ensure that our actions promote the human dignity of each person. In this unit you will examine situations where human dignity is not respected.

Chapter 1:   Rights and responsibilities in the community
Chapter 2:   Human dignity
Chapter 3:   Human needs
Chapter 4:   Access to food and water: A global challenge

Unit 2   HUMAN RIGHTS INSTRUMENTS

Human rights instruments are key documents that seek to protect and promote human rights. You will examine some key human rights documents and consider how these apply to your life. You will explore ways you can take responsibility for defending your own human rights and those of others.

Chapter 5:   Human rights timeline
Chapter 6:   Human rights champions
Chapter 7:   Human rights instruments
Chapter 8:   Classification of human rights
Chapter 9:   Human rights conflicts and abuses
Chapter 10: Taking responsibility for human rights

Rights and responsibilities in the community

Learning outcomes

By the end of this chapter you will understand what it means to be human and live in a community with rights and responsibilities.

Key words

- Diversity
- Human dignity
- Human rights
- Universal
- Responsibilities
- Communities
- Sense of belonging
- Inclusive
- Community spirit
- School community
- Wellbeing
- Local community
- Active citizens
- Community action

Key skills you will use in this chapter

- ✓ Being Creative
- ✓ Being Literate
- ✓ Being Numerate
- ✓ Communicating
- ✓ Managing Information and Thinking
- ✓ Managing Myself
- ✓ Staying Well
- ✓ Working with Others

Wellbeing indicators in this chapter

Being human

Despite the fact that almost 8 billion people inhabit our planet, every single human being is unique. Being unique means that you are one of a kind and different from others. These differences mean that there is diversity among all human beings.

You don't have to look far to find **diversity** – it is all around you. Look at your classmates. They all look different and have different personalities, interests and talents. Diversity is also evident in the local community, in Ireland and in the wider world, where differences exist in terms of gender, age, religion, race and culture. Diversity makes our world a more beautiful, colourful and interesting place to live.

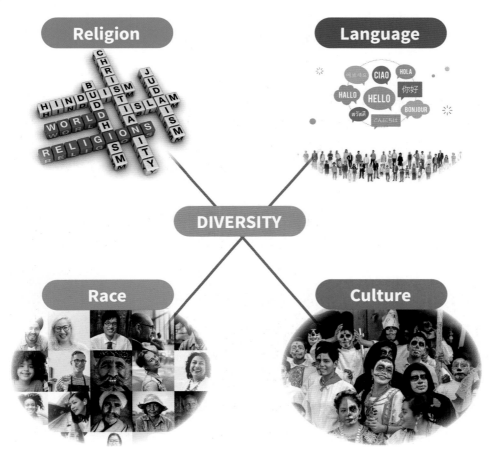

Human dignity

When we respect difference, we are recognising that every person is valuable. Every person, no matter how different, is entitled to **human dignity**. Individuals can live their lives with dignity if their basic needs are met. This means having enough to eat or drink, a place to call home and feeling respected and valued by others.

Human rights

Simply because you are human, you are also entitled to **human rights**. Rights are freedoms that enable every person to develop fully as a human being. Human rights are **universal**. This means they apply to every person, without exception. Human rights and human dignity are closely linked because human dignity is the foundation for human rights. When our rights are protected and respected, we can live our lives with dignity. When rights are not respected or are taken away, individuals and groups can suffer a loss of human dignity.

Can you think of some rights every person is entitled to?

Responsibilities

Responsibilities go hand in hand with rights. By acting responsibly and making the right decisions, we can ensure that our rights and the rights of others are respected and protected. It is also important that we act in a responsible manner towards our environment so that it can be enjoyed by future generations.

⊘ Being Literate
⊘ Managing Information
   and Thinking
⊘ Managing Myself

Questions

Kofi Annan was Secretary General of the United Nations from 1997 to 2006. The following is an excerpt from a speech he made on Human Rights Day, 10 December 1997 (the 50th anniversary of the Universal Declaration of Human Rights). Read it and answer the questions that follow.

'Human rights are what make us human. They are the principles by which we create the sacred home for human dignity. It is the universality of human rights that gives them their strength. It endows them with the power to cross any border, climb any wall, defy any force.'

1   According to Kofi Annan, what makes us human?

2   What gives human rights their strength?

3   What is meant by 'it endows them with the power to cross any border, climb any wall, defy any force'?

Community

Humans are social beings. We have a need to relate to and connect with other people. We also need to be accepted and valued by others. For these reasons, humans tend to organise themselves into **communities**. A community can be described as:

🌐 A group of people who have something in common with each other

🌐 A group of people who share a common place.

A **sense of belonging** is important to community members. This is the sense of connectedness that an individual has to their community. It is important that all communities are **inclusive**. Inclusive communities respect difference and diversity and ensure that nobody is excluded in the life of the community.

The most successful communities have something called **community spirit**. This is the willingness of community members to participate in the life of the community, co-operate with each other and make their community a better place for all.

You are a member of many communities. Let's look at some examples.

School community

The family community

Local communities/ neighbourhoods

Sporting communities

The Irish community

Rights and responsibilities in the school community

When you started in your secondary school, you became a member of a new community. The **school community** is not just a building – it is also a set of relationships between students, teachers, parents, school staff and the wider community. Every member of the school community has certain rights and is entitled to the protection of these rights.

Think, pair and share

- Being Literate
- Communicating
- Managing Information and Thinking
- Managing Myself
- Working with Others

Think about the rights all members of the school community are entitled to – students, teachers, the principal and parents.

Write down one right to which each of these members of the school community is entitled. Now listen to your partner's views. Are there similarities or differences? Decide on the information you will share with the class group. Use the table in your reflective journal to write down your ideas.

One of the most important rights is the right to an education. However, members of the school community also have responsibilities. As a student, you must take responsibility for your education. You have a responsibility to get to school on time, to have your books, copies and equipment, to complete your homework and to make an effort in school.

Not all members of the school community have the same responsibilities.

⊕ Teachers have a responsibility to ensure that their students receive the best possible education.

⊕ Parents have a responsibility to make sure that their children attend school.

⊕ The school principal has a responsibility to ensure that students are safe and that school rules are followed. The principal is also responsible for the **wellbeing** of those within the school community.

Rights and responsibilities in the local community

A **local community** can be described as a group of people who interact with each other and share a common environment. Local communities are made up of a broad range of people. Although all community members have the same rights, sometimes they have different responsibilities towards the community.

Let's meet some community members. Study the profiles of each community member. Each profile will state a right to which that person is entitled. In your copybook, write down one responsibility of that community member.

Profile ❶

John passed his driving test one month ago. He has just bought his first car and is looking forward to driving it.

John has a right to own and drive his car. What does John have a responsibility to do?

Profile ❷

Margaret owns the local shop. She has run it for the past twenty years. She sells newspapers, confectionery and cigarettes.

Margaret has a right to own and run her business in the local community. What does Margaret have a responsibility to do?

Profile ③

Pat owns a mixed farm just outside the village. He sometimes uses pesticides on his crops to ensure that they survive. There is a small stream that runs through Pat's farm.

Pat has a right to use pesticides on his crops. What does Pat have a responsibility to do?

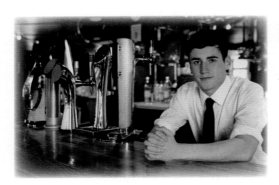

Profile ④

Seán owns and runs the local bar, which is located in the middle of a housing estate. Every Friday night is DJ night and the music can get quite loud.

Seán has a right to own and run his bar. What does Seán have a responsibility to do?

Profile ⑤

Suzanne is a local property developer. She buys houses and land to develop them and make a profit. She has recently purchased an area of wasteland on the edge of town. She wants to build high-rise apartments on the site. She has applied for planning permission. All the local people are unhappy about this, as a high-rise development would block their view of the mountains.

Suzanne has a right to develop local houses and land. What does Suzanne have a responsibility to do?

Group activity

- ⊘ Being Literate
- ⊘ Communicating
- ⊘ Managing Information and Thinking
- ⊘ Managing Myself
- ⊘ Working with Others

Divide into groups. In your group, name three other key members of your local community. Discuss each member's role in the community. Write down one right and one responsibility for each community member.

Active citizenship in the community

People who strive to make their communities a better place are often called **active citizens**. Active citizens are those who act in a responsible way towards other members of the community.

An active citizen is somebody who:

Is aware of their rights and responsibilities

Respects the rights and human dignity of others

Takes action on issues that affect them and their community

Participates in the life of the community

Takes care of the local environment and protects it for future generations

Community action

Sometimes communities face issues or challenges that can affect the wellbeing of community members. Instead of brushing these challenges under the carpet, community groups work together to address these challenges and take action to highlight or resolve them. This is called **community action**.

The River Dodder in Dublin, with the Aviva Stadium in the background

The Dodder is a river that runs through South Dublin. The Dodder Action Group was set up to preserve and protect the river as an important local amenity. This group of active citizens organises monthly clean-ups of the river and educates the local community about conservation (protection) and the ecology of the Dodder (the relationship of living things with the river).

Connect and communicate

- ⊘ Being Literate
- ⊘ Communicating
- ⊘ Managing Information and Thinking
- ⊘ Managing Myself
- ⊘ Working with Others

Get in contact with a community action group in your local area to find out the following information:

1. Why the action group was set up
2. What challenges/issues/problems they are trying to address or resolve
3. Actions or projects they have undertaken to address these issues

Group activity

Divide the class into six groups. Each group will choose one of the photographs below. Each photograph represents a community issue. Discuss what issue the photograph is highlighting and answer the questions that follow.

- ⊘ Being Creative
- ⊘ Being Literate
- ⊘ Communicating
- ⊘ Managing Information and Thinking
- ⊘ Managing Myself
- ⊘ Working with Others

Photograph 1

Photograph 2

Photograph 3

Photograph 4

Photograph 5

Photograph 6

1   What issue is being highlighted by your photograph?

2   Name one action your community could undertake to resolve this issue.

3   Describe how you would organise that action.

Citizens' rights and responsibilities

As an Irish citizen, you are entitled to certain rights and the protection of these rights. Some of these rights include:

- 🌐 The right to hold an Irish passport
- 🌐 The right to own property
- 🌐 The right to vote in elections if you are over eighteen
- 🌐 The right to marry.

Can you think of some other rights Irish citizens are entitled to?

As an Irish citizen, you also have duties or responsibilities. These include:

- 🌐 The responsibility to vote in elections
- 🌐 The responsibility to respect the law
- 🌐 The responsibility to respect and protect the environment.

Can you think of some other responsibilities of Irish citizens?

The Irish government also has certain duties or responsibilities towards its citizens. These responsibilities include:

- 🌐 Protecting and promoting the rights of citizens
- 🌐 Protecting and promoting the welfare of citizens
- 🌐 Making laws that are fair and just
- 🌐 Accepting the outcome of elections
- 🌐 Providing services to citizens.

Can you think of others?

Research

As an Irish citizen, you need to be aware of your rights and responsibilities.

To find out more about your rights and entitlements, log on to the Citizens Information website. This website provides information and advice on the rights of Irish citizens.

- ⊘ Being Creative
- ⊘ Communicating
- ⊘ Managing Information and Thinking
- ⊘ Staying Well

Take action!

With your class group, create a class charter of rights and responsibilities.

This charter will raise awareness about the importance of rights in your class and the responsibility to respect the rights of others.

- ⊘ Being Creative
- ⊘ Being Literate
- ⊘ Managing Information and Thinking
- ⊘ Managing Myself
- ⊘ Staying Well
- ⊘ Working with Others

OUR CLASS CHARTER

We have a right to...

We have a responsibility to...

Don't forget to complete your reflections in your reflective journal.

Chapter 2

UNIT 1

HUMAN DIGNITY:
THE BASIS FOR HUMAN RIGHTS

Human dignity

Learning outcomes

By the end of this chapter you will have examined situations where human dignity is not respected. You will be able to create a visual representation to communicate a situation where human dignity is not respected.

Key skills you will use in this chapter

- ✓ Being Creative
- ✓ Being Literate
- ✓ Being Numerate
- ✓ Communicating
- ✓ Managing Information and Thinking
- ✓ Managing Myself
- ✓ Staying Well
- ✓ Working with Others

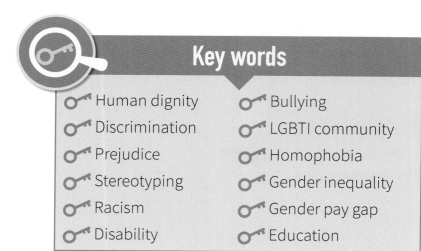

Key words

- Human dignity
- Discrimination
- Prejudice
- Stereotyping
- Racism
- Disability
- Bullying
- LGBTI community
- Homophobia
- Gender inequality
- Gender pay gap
- Education

Wellbeing indicators in this chapter

Human dignity

Video Dignity – Little things make a big difference

Every person, without exception, is entitled to **human dignity**. Human dignity is not only a right, it is also the foundation for all other human rights. In other words, all human rights ensure that every person can live their life with dignity.

What do we mean when we talk about human dignity? The visual below outlines the factors that enable an individual to live their life with dignity.

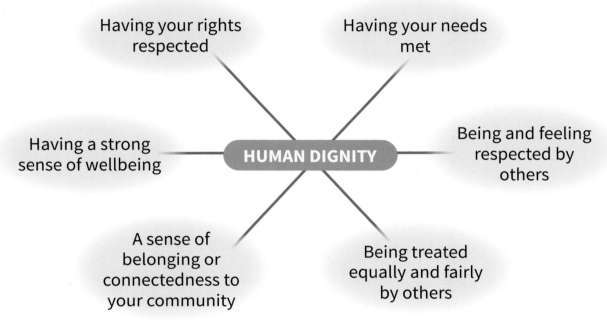

Having your rights respected

Having your needs met

Having a strong sense of wellbeing

HUMAN DIGNITY

Being and feeling respected by others

A sense of belonging or connectedness to your community

Being treated equally and fairly by others

Look at the two pictures opposite. How do you think the people are feeling in the picture on the left? Why are they feeling that way? How do you think the people in the picture on the right are feeling? Why are they feeling that way?

People ranked by skill

People ranked by dignity

Think, pair and share

Think about human dignity. What is your understanding of it?

⊘ Being Literate
⊘ Communicating
⊘ Managing Information and Thinking
⊘ Managing Myself
⊘ Working with Others

In your reflective journal, write your definition of human dignity. Now turn to your partner and listen to their definition of human dignity. As a pair, decide on a definition that best describes human dignity. Share this definition with the class group. Use the table in your reflective journal to write down your ideas.

When human dignity is not respected

Human dignity is important because it enables us to develop fully as human beings and to lead happy, healthy lives. When human dignity is respected, we can have a strong sense of wellbeing.

Unfortunately, human dignity is not always respected. As a result, an individual or group can suffer a loss of human dignity. Sometimes our words, actions, behaviours and attitudes can impact on the human dignity of others. A loss of human dignity can have serious consequences for individuals and groups.

We will now explore some situations where human dignity is not respected.

Discrimination

In Chapter 1 you learned about diversity and the importance of respecting difference. Sometimes people are uncomfortable or afraid of diversity. This causes them to treat others differently and sometimes unfairly.

In Ireland, **discrimination** occurs when individuals or groups are treated differently or unfairly because of factors such as age, gender, religion, disability, civil status (married, divorced, single, etc.), family status, membership of the Traveller community or sexual orientation.

Unfortunately, many individuals and groups experience discrimination and therefore suffer a loss of human dignity. The following people often experience discrimination.

Refugees and asylum seekers

Homeless people

Members of the Traveller community

People with disabilites

Older people

Members of the LGBTI community

Group activity

Divide the class into five groups. Study the media headlines below.

Each headline refers to a situation where somebody was discriminated against. Each group should choose **one** of these headlines. When you have chosen your headline, discuss with your group what may have happened in each situation. Write a media report about that situation. In your report, describe how that situation led to a loss of human dignity.

- ⊘ Being Creative
- ⊘ Being Literate
- ⊘ Communicating
- ⊘ Managing Information and Thinking
- ⊘ Managing Myself
- ⊘ Working with Others

Man injured in racial attack

Traveller refused entry to hotel

Gay couple refused the right to adopt a child

Woman loses job because she was pregnant

Child refused school place because of her religion

Prejudice and stereotyping

Prejudice and stereotyping are two forms of discrimination.

Prejudice occurs when individuals or groups are pre-judged. Sometimes we pre-judge individuals or groups in a negative way because of their age, how they look, how they speak or because they are members of a particular group. Prejudice means we make assumptions about people without getting to know them as individuals. Prejudice is wrong because it can deprive individuals of their right to be treated equally, which can lead to a loss of human dignity.

Can you think of some groups in Irish society who experience prejudice?

Group activity

Do the lifeboat dilemma activity in your reflective journal.

- ✓ Being Literate
- ✓ Communicating
- ✓ Managing Information and Thinking
- ✓ Managing Myself
- ✓ Working with Others

Stereotyping occurs when we label a group of people, usually in a negative way. When we stereotype a group of people, we believe that members of this group are all the same. This was the case for many years in the film industry. Irish people were often depicted as drunks or lovers of fist-fights. Do you think this stereotype is accurate? Why or why not? How does this stereotype make you feel?

Here are some examples of negative stereotypes:

🌐 Refugees come to Ireland to get free houses.

🌐 All Travellers are criminals.

🌐 Women can't drive.

🌐 People on social welfare just don't want to work.

Can you think of some others?

It is important that we don't stereotype groups of people. Instead, we should get to know members from different groups and recognise that every person is different and unique.

We will now explore some further examples of discrimination and how it can lead to a loss of human dignity.

Discrimination issue Racism

Racism is a form of discrimination. It is the false belief that some races of people or ethnic groups are better than others. It is based on fear: fear of the unknown or fear of the 'other'.

Racism can happen when:

🌐 People make jokes or negative comments about a race or ethnic group.

🌐 People are verbally abused in connection to race or ethnicity.

🌐 People are physically attacked because of their colour or accent.

🌐 People are refused access to goods and services because they are different.

Sometimes racism can be hidden or less obvious. An example of this is an employer not giving a job to a qualified individual because of their race or ethnic background.

Racism should not be tolerated. It deprives individuals and groups of their human dignity. It deprives the person or people being racist of their human dignity too.

John's story

I have been living in Ireland for the past five years. I moved here to take a job in the IT sector. I really like Ireland. Although the weather isn't great, it's a good place to live.

For the most part, people have been really nice and welcoming. However, the words and actions of others have made me feel different and sometimes worthless.

I live a fair distance from my workplace, so I have to get the bus to work every day. A number of times I have been verbally abused by other bus passengers. People have called me names. I am often told to go back home to where I came from. There is nothing worse than twenty or thirty faces looking at you on a bus while some idiot hurls racist abuse at you. The sad thing about this is that no one has ever defended me on the bus. Racial name-calling really upsets me and makes me feel like I don't belong. It's getting to the point where I don't want to take the bus any more. I have often walked the five-mile journey to and from work in the lashing rain to avoid the prospect of been called racist names. I wish racism would just go away!

? Questions

1 How does racism affect John's human dignity? Explain your answer.

2 Why, do you think, does no one defend him on the bus?

3 John wishes racism would go away.
In your reflective journal, design an anti-racism T-shirt that encourages people to stand up against racism.

Fighting back against racism

Racism is not a new phenomenon. A study of history will reveal many examples of racism targeted at various races and ethnic groups. Examples include the slave trade in the United States, Apartheid in South Africa and the genocide of the Jewish people during World War II. Unfortunately, racism has not gone away – it is still a huge issue today. There is a growing number of organisations that have been set up to fight back against racism. These groups raise awareness about racism and organise anti-racist campaigns, protests and educational programmes to highlight the injustices caused by racism and racist behaviours.

Black Lives Matter

Black Lives Matter (BLM) is a global social movement that was formed in the United States in 2013. This movement is dedicated to fighting racism and violence against black communities. BLM was set up in response to the killing of a young, unarmed African American man by a neighbourhood watch volunteer, simply because the young man looked 'suspicious'.

Two young women hold banners at a protest in Vancouver, Canada, in 2020

The killer was later acquitted of the murder in court. Many felt that justice was not served. A string of protests against the court's decision took place. Since then, the

BLM movement has grown. The BLM message is that society needs to value the lives of black people as much as it values the lives of white people.

The BLM movement raises awareness of the many ways in which people in black communities are treated unfairly in society – one example being police brutality. BLM fights racism by organising letter-writing campaigns and non-violent protests. BLM also celebrates the work of black artists, writers and innovators.

BLM achieved worldwide attention in 2020 in the aftermath of the death of George Floyd. Floyd, an unarmed, black man, was pronounced dead after a Minneapolis police officer knelt on his neck for over nine minutes, despite Floyd's repeated protests that he couldn't breathe. The killing was captured on video and created shockwaves around the world. Floyd's death at the hands of the police triggered huge anti-racism demonstrations in the US and around the world and BLM gained numerous supporters. In 2021 the police officer in question was found guilty of the murder of George Floyd.

Show Racism the Red Card

Show Racism the Red Card is another organisation that seeks to combat racism. This organisation enlists high-profile footballers and sportspeople to convey its anti-racism message. Many sportspeople, particularly footballers, have been subjected to racist chants and behaviours from spectators. In response, Show Racism the Red Card has organised many campaigns and

High-profile footballers often support campaigns that tackle racism in sport

workshops to educate young people about racism and its effects on individuals and communities.

Connect and communicate

Find out about other organisations that educate people about racism and aim to eliminate it.

Contact one of these organisations and find out about some of their campaigns that aim to eliminate racism.

- ⊘ Being Literate
- ⊘ Communicating
- ⊘ Managing Information and Thinking
- ⊘ Managing Myself
- ⊘ Working with Others

Discrimination issue ❷ Disability

We live in a society that views able-bodied people as the norm. As a result, people with disabilities are often discriminated against. There are many

forms of **disability**, including physical, sensory, intellectual and mental disabilities. People with disabilities often experience a range of barriers that prevent them from accessing employment, basic services and the ability to participate fully in society. These barriers include attitudinal, communication and physical barriers.

Attitudinal barriers

Attitudes towards people with a disability can sometimes be negative. Some people view disability as a personal tragedy or something to be prevented or cured. Others assume that quality of life is poor because of an individual's disability. Negative attitudes like these create further barriers for those with disabilities. A positive attitude involves not seeing disability as a shortcoming, but rather realising that disability occurs when an individual's needs are not met by their physical and social environment. Some people don't make eye contact with a person using a wheelchair. If the wheelchair user is with a carer who is standing, some people will talk only to the carer and act as if the wheelchair user is invisible! How would you feel if someone acted like you were not there?

Communication barriers

Individuals with sensory or intellectual disabilities often come up against communication barriers in their everyday lives. People who are visually impaired may need books and notices with larger print. For instance, people who are blind may need to access Braille (Braille is a system of touch reading consisting of raised dots).

Sometimes larger-print texts and Braille are not made available to those with a visual impairment, so everyday things like going to the supermarket, for example, can prove a huge challenge.

Physical barriers

The physical environment can provide barriers and challenges to those with disabilities, especially those with impaired mobility. Many buildings, shops and vehicles are designed for able-bodied people. They don't have ramps or lifts and don't cater for wheelchair users.

Making a difference

Sometimes our actions, although not deliberate, can create obstacles or barriers for those who have impaired mobility. To raise awareness about this issue, Dublin City Council launched the 'Make Way Dublin' campaign in 2017. This campaign aimed to educate householders and businesses about their responsibility to make their environments more accessible for those with disabilities.

Here are some ways in which everyday actions can create obstacles for wheelchair users or people with impaired mobility:

- 🌐 Parking a car so it partly or completely blocks the footpath
- 🌐 Letting a hedge grow onto the footpath
- 🌐 Locking a bike to a lamp post
- 🌐 Businesses putting up sandwich boards on the street.

- ✓ Being Creative
- ✓ Being Literate
- ✓ Managing Information and Thinking
- ✓ Managing Myself
- ✓ Staying Well

? Questions

1. List four other ways in which our everyday actions can create major difficulties for people with disabilities.

2. If you see obstacles for wheelchair users or people with impaired mobility, what can you do?

3. Can you think of one action your class could undertake to make students in your school aware of how simple actions can make a difference in the lives of people with disabilities?

Human dignity: When rights are not respected

In the last chapter you learned that rights are one of the things that make us human. Every person, without exception, is entitled to human rights. When rights are not respected or when they are abused or denied, a loss of human dignity can occur. You will now explore three situations where rights are not being respected. You will also examine how these situations can lead to a loss of human dignity.

Human dignity issue ❶ Bullying

Every person has the right to feel safe and secure. **Bullying** can deny an individual this important right. Bullying involves repeated and unwanted negative behaviour directed at an individual or group. Bullying is a serious issue not only in schools, but also in youth clubs, sports clubs and workplaces.

Bullying can make life very difficult for people. Young people who have experienced bullying in school have reported that it made them physically sick, anxious, depressed and reluctant to attend school at all. Bullying can deny human dignity and should never be tolerated.

Forms of bullying

1. **Physical bullying:** Physically hurting or threatening another person. It can involve punching, kicking, hitting, pushing or deliberately trying to trip someone up.

2. **Verbal bullying:** Calling another person names, insulting, humiliating or teasing another person.

3. **Non-verbal bullying:** Making faces or gestures at another person.

4 **Social and emotional bullying:** Spreading rumours about, deliberately ignoring, excluding or threatening another person.

5 **Cyberbullying:** Using social media or text messages to humiliate, embarrass, tell lies about, threaten or spread rumours about another person. It can also involve posting photos or videos that set out to embarrass or humiliate another person.

6 **Homophobic bullying:** This form of bullying is aimed at members of the **LGBTI community**. LGBTI stands for

L = Lesbian

G = Gay

B = Bisexual

T =Transgender

I = Intersex (this refers to individuals born with both male and female reproductive organs)

Homophobia refers to negative attitudes towards members of the LGBTI community. Members of this community often experience homophobic bullying. Victims of homophobic bullying have been physically assaulted, verbally abused, intimidated or bullied because of their sexual orientation.

How to deal with bullying

What to do if you are being bullied	What to do if you witness others being bullied
⊕ Tell someone – don't suffer in silence. Tell a responsible adult, such as a parent, teacher or sports coach. ⊕ If you are being bullied on social media, don't respond to the bully online. Block or unfriend the bully. Report the bully to the social media site.	⊕ Don't join in with the bullies. ⊕ Report your concerns to a responsible adult. ⊕ Reassure and be a friend to the person experiencing bullying.

- Being Literate
- Managing Information and Thinking
- Managing Myself

Individual activity

Study the photographs below. Each picture represents a different form of bullying.

Match each photograph with the type of bullying involved. Copy the table below into your copybook and complete this activity.

Picture A

Picture B

Picture C

Picture D

Picture	Type of bullying
A	
B	
C	
D	

Human dignity issue ❷
Gender inequality

Every person has the right to be treated equally. Despite this, many groups of people experience inequality. One such group is women. Many women in Ireland and throughout the world experience **gender inequality**. This means that men and women are treated differently. Although women's rights have improved over the last century, many women today don't have the same rights and

opportunities as men. This makes women feel disrespected and undervalued. Women can feel like second-class citizens and can experience a lack of self-worth. Gender inequality can therefore lead to a loss of human dignity.

Facts on gender inequality

- 🌐 Women are vastly under-represented in political life around the world. Most of the positions of power are held by men. In Ireland in 2016, only 22% of all TDs were women. Ireland has never had a female taoiseach.

- 🌐 More than two-thirds of the world's illiterate population is female. In some societies girls are not allowed to go to school.

- 🌐 In Switzerland, women did not have the right to vote in national elections until 1971. Men started voting there in the year 1291.

- 🌐 In 2016, only 14% of Irish companies had a female chief executive or head of operations.

- 🌐 Women in Saudi Arabia were not permitted to drive a car until 2018.

- 🌐 Four out of five victims of human trafficking are girls.

- 🌐 More than 40% of women in sub-Saharan Africa and South Asia are married before their eighteenth birthday. Many marriages are arranged and the bride has no choice in who she marries.

- 🌐 Until the law was changed in 1973, Irish women working in the civil service had to give up their job when they got married.

- 🌐 In some countries, women are not permitted to own land or property. In Sudan, Tanzania and Lesotho, for example, control of property and land usually goes to the oldest male in the household.

The gender pay gap

Gender inequality can exist in the amount of money women earn in comparison to men. In some situations, women get paid less than men who do the same job. In addition, men are more likely to hold higher-paying managerial positions in companies. The difference between the average gross earnings of female and male employees is referred to as the **gender pay gap**.

GENDER PAY GAP ACROSS EUROPE

🎓 EDUCATION

There is a gender pay gap even though women do better at school and university than men.

83% 👩

of young women reach at least upper secondary school in the EU compared to

77.5% 👨 of men.

60%

of EU university graduates are women.

💼 EMPLOYMENT

The employment rate for women in Europe is

62.4% 👩 compared to

74.6% 👨 for men aged 20–64.

Most of the part-time workers in the EU are women:

36% VS. 9.5%

This has a negative impact on women's careers, training opportunities, pension rights and unemployment.

🐷 POVERTY

The gender pay gap can result in poverty over time.

23% 👩

of women over 65 are at risk of poverty compared to

17% 👨 of men.

On average, women in the EU earn

16.2%

less per hour than men.

LARGEST AND SMALLEST PAY GAPS IN THE EU BY COUNTRY

⚙️ CAUSES OF THE GENDER GAP

- ⚙ Discrimination in the workplace
- ⚙ Workplace practices and pay systems
- ⚙ Undervaluing women's work and skills
- ⚙ Gender roles and traditions

13.9% Ireland

22.2% Germany

4.5% Poland

27.3% Estonia

23.7% Austria

21% Czech Rep.

20.5% Slovakia

8.7% Lux.

2.3% Slovenia

22% Greece

5.8% Italy

<10%

Slovenia, Poland, Italy and Luxembourg

>20%

Slovakia, Czech Republic, Greece, Germany, Austria and Estonia

Source: European Commission

❓ Questions

- ✓ Being Literate
- ✓ Being Numerate
- ✓ Managing Information and Thinking
- ✓ Managing Myself

Video Irish Human Rights and Equality Commission – Gender equality and women's rights in Ireland

Study the infographic above. It shows the gender pay gap throughout Europe. Now answer the questions that follow.

1 According to the infographic, what are the causes of the gender pay gap?

2 What percentage of university graduates are women? Are you surprised by this figure? Give a reason for your answer.

3 What country has the largest gender pay gap?

4 What country has the smallest gender pay gap?

5 On average, how much more do men earn in comparison to women?

6 Describe how the gender pay gap can impact on human dignity.

Questions

Study this image, which highlights gender stereotyping. In your copybook, answer the questions that follow.

1 Describe what is happening in the photo.

2 Describe one other way in which men or women are gender stereotyped.

3 How does gender stereotyping affect an individual's human dignity?

Human dignity issue ❸ Education

Education is a basic human right. It is through education that we can make a better life for ourselves and become more knowledgeable and powerful. It is also through education that many can break the cycle of poverty. Despite this, millions of children worldwide are denied this right.

Education around the world

- 🌐 Fifty-nine million children of primary school age across the globe don't attend school.

- 🌐 Sixty-five million children of secondary school age don't attend school.

- 🌐 War, conflict and natural disasters have disrupted the education of more than 75 million children worldwide.

- 🌐 A child whose mother can read is more likely to survive past the age of five.

- 🌐 Over 15 million girls around the world will never have the chance to attend primary school or learn to read or write.

- 🌐 There are about 168 million child labourers in the world. Most of these children don't attend school.

- 🌐 Two-thirds of the illiterate people in the world are women.

- 🌐 The African continent has areas with less than 50% literacy rates.

Being Literate
Being Numerate
Managing Information and Thinking
Managing Myself

? Questions

1   Who is more likely to be educated: boys or girls? Why, do you think, is that?

2   How many child labourers exist in the world today? Why, do you think, do they not attend school?

3   What continent has areas with less than a 50% literacy rate?

Fatima's story

Fatima lives in Nigeria with her brother and her parents.

Her father is a farmer and struggles to find enough food for the family to eat. They currently live in a house belonging to another family. Without money to pay for school uniforms, books and other materials, Fatima is unable to go to school.

'My name is Fatima and I am ten years old. I live with my three-year-old brother Umaru and my mother and father in a friend's house.

'Every morning I say my prayers and help my mother by collecting water, cooking and doing other chores around the house. When we have onions to sell I go out hawking (selling), but when there are none I stay at home. I don't go to school because my parents are poor. It makes me feel unhappy that I am not going to school.

'My friends are called Fadila and Ummi. I feel so bad when I watch my friends walking off to school. I would love to join them instead of going out hawking. If I did go to school one day, I would like to work in a hospital.'

Fatima's parents never had the chance to go to school. Fatima's mother, Hadiza, says: 'I would like Fatima and her brother to go to school, but we cannot provide for it. If they become educated I think their life will be better.'

Source: Send My Friend to School

Questions

1   Why does Fatima not go to school?

2   In your opinion, do her parents have a choice with regard to sending her to school? Explain your answer.

3   In addition to the right to an education, what other rights do you think Fatima's family lacks?

- ✓ Being Literate
- ✓ Managing Information and Thinking
- ✓ Managing Myself

Think, pair and share

Think about what this quote means. Think of ways in which education can change the world.

- ✓ Being Literate
- ✓ Communicating
- ✓ Managing Information and Thinking
- ✓ Managing Myself
- ✓ Working with Others

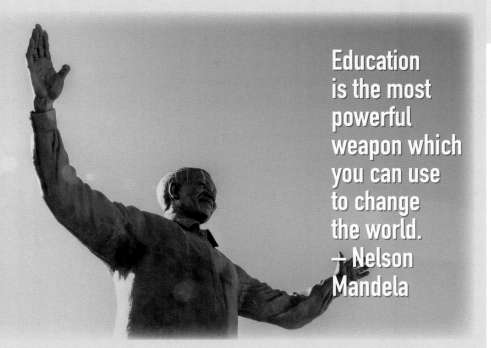

Education is the most powerful weapon which you can use to change the world. — Nelson Mandela

Now turn to your partner, listen to their ideas and make a note of them. Decide what information you will share with the class group. Use the table in your reflective journal to write down your ideas.

Connect and communicate

- ✓ Being Creative
- ✓ Being Literate
- ✓ Communicating
- ✓ Managing Information and Thinking
- ✓ Managing Myself
- ✓ Staying Well

Find out about a human rights organisation at home or abroad that campaigns for the right to education. Connect with that organisation and find out how it promotes education as a fundamental human right.

Take action!

- ✓ Being Creative
- ✓ Communicating
- ✓ Managing Information and Thinking
- ✓ Managing Myself

In this chapter you have explored situations where human dignity was not respected.

Create a visual representation to communicate one of these situations. Your visual can be a picture, poster or infographic or it can be a PowerPoint presentation or video.

Don't forget to complete your reflections in your reflective journal.

Learning outcomes

By the end of this chapter you will be able to explain the hierarchy of human needs and how this relates to human rights.

Key skills you will use in this chapter

- ✓ **Being Creative**
- ✓ **Being Literate**
- ✓ **Being Numerate**
- ✓ **Communicating**
- ✓ **Managing Information and Thinking**
- ✓ **Managing Myself**
- ✓ **Staying Well**
- ✓ **Working with Others**

Key words

- ⚷ Human needs
- ⚷ Hierarchy
- ⚷ Survival needs
- ⚷ Safety, security and protection needs
- ⚷ Love and belonging needs
- ⚷ Self-esteem needs
- ⚷ Full potential
- ⚷ Consumer society

Wellbeing indicators in this chapter

Human needs

Everyone has **human needs** that must be met if they are to survive, feel safe and live happy and healthy lives. When an individual's needs are met, they can live their lives with dignity.

Maslow's hierarchy of human needs

Abraham Maslow, an American psychologist, developed a **hierarchy** of human needs. A hierarchy is a system that ranks things in order of importance. Maslow used a pyramid to explain this hierarchy. He believed that once our most basic needs are met, we can reach the next level of needs and so on.

Abraham Maslow (1908–1970)

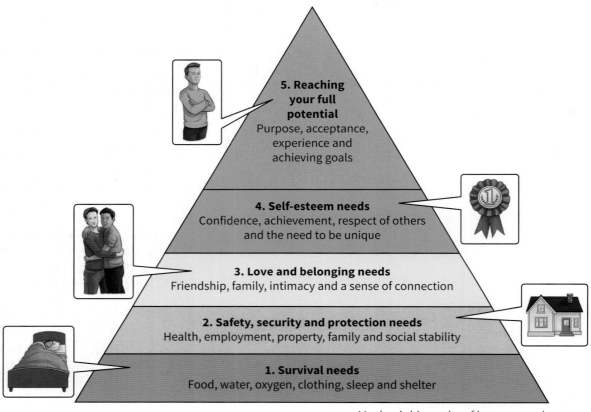

5. Reaching your full potential
Purpose, acceptance, experience and achieving goals

4. Self-esteem needs
Confidence, achievement, respect of others and the need to be unique

3. Love and belonging needs
Friendship, family, intimacy and a sense of connection

2. Safety, security and protection needs
Health, employment, property, family and social stability

1. Survival needs
Food, water, oxygen, clothing, sleep and shelter

Maslow's hierarchy of human needs

① Survival needs

Survival needs are our most basic needs. They are the things we need to survive. These needs include food, water, oxygen, clothing, sleep and shelter.

② Safety, security and protection needs

Safety, security and protection needs enable us to stay safe and feel secure and protected. Examples of these needs include living in a safe and secure environment and having access to healthcare and employment.

③ Love and belonging needs

Human beings need to be loved, to be accepted and to feel connected to others. These needs include friendship, **love and a sense of belonging**.

④ Self-esteem needs

Every person has the need to feel valued, appreciated and respected by others. When these needs are met, individuals have self-worth, self-confidence and **self-esteem**.

⑤ The need to develop your full potential

People want to be the best they can be. Everybody needs meaning and purpose in their lives. Setting personal goals and attempting to reach these goals enables individuals to develop their **full potential**.

Think, pair and share

⊘ Being Literate
⊘ Communicating
⊘ Managing Information and Thinking
⊘ Managing Myself
⊘ Working with Others

Not having your needs met can have a negative impact on your health, happiness and wellbeing.

Think about the consequences for you of not having the following needs met:

- Survival needs
- Safety, security and protection needs
- Love and belonging needs
- Self-esteem needs
- The need to develop to your full potential.

Now turn to your partner and share your thoughts with them. Are they similar or different? Now share those thoughts with the class group. Use the table in your reflective journal to write down your ideas.

Need or want?

It is important that we don't confuse needs and wants. Unlike needs, wants are things that we desire or would like to have, but they are not necessary to our survival.

We live in a **consumer society** that encourages us to buy goods that we don't need. There is also a high value placed on owning many things. Every day we are bombarded with advertisements from companies trying to get us to buy their products. These advertisements often persuade consumers to believe that the products are needs instead of wants. In your reflective journal, create your own hierarchy of human needs. You may use words, pictures, icons or drawings to represent each set of needs.

Group activity

Divide into groups of three or four. Look at the images below.

In your group, discuss whether each image represents a need or a want.

- ⊘ Being Literate
- ⊘ Communicating
- ⊘ Managing Information and Thinking
- ⊘ Managing Myself
- ⊘ Working with Others

Debate

Organise a walking debate on the following topic:

 'In the twenty-first century, Irish teenagers want more than they need.'

Having completed the debate, has your opinion remained the same or has it changed? Can you explain why?

- ⊘ Being Creative
- ⊘ Being Literate
- ⊘ Communicating
- ⊘ Managing Information and Thinking
- ⊘ Managing Myself
- ⊘ Working with Others

Meet the Gallagher family

The Gallagher family is a typical twenty-first-century Irish family. They live just outside Westport in Co. Mayo. Brendan and Evelyn Gallagher have been married for twenty years and have four children. John is nineteen and has just started college; Maeve is fifteen and is studying for her JCSA; Éabha is ten and is attending the local primary school; and Luke is five and a half and has started Junior Infants.

We asked each member of the Gallagher family what the needs of a family living in Ireland are. Let's look at their answers.

Evelyn Gallagher

I think having a house to live in and food on the table are essential. I think water and sanitation are important too. Electricity helps us to cook, wash and refrigerate food. Clothes are also important. It can get very cold in Westport during the winter, so we need warm clothes. On a more personal level, I think it is important that our children feel loved and valued by Brendan and me.

Brendan Gallagher

I agree with Evelyn. A roof over our heads and food on the table are the important needs. I have a full-time job and Evelyn works part time, which means we have money coming in every month. Since my job is 30 km away I need a car to go to and from work. My work also involves travelling between towns in the west, so for me, a car is something I need.

John Gallagher

I've just started college, so I think education is an important need. Mam and Dad always made sure I went to school and they place a high value on education. I have to travel to and from Galway every day for college, so public transport is important to me. I would love to have my own car, but this is more of a want than a need at the moment.

Maeve Gallagher

I broke my leg recently playing a camogie match and I had to go to the hospital in Castlebar, where they put my leg in a cast, so healthcare for me is an important need. It's important that we can go to doctors and hospitals when we need them.

Éabha Gallagher

I think having a mobile phone is an important need. Having a phone helps you be in touch with your friends. I think tablets and laptops are important too. You can use social media sites and see what your friends are up to. You can't use any of these things if you don't have wi-fi, so wi-fi is an important need as far as I'm concerned!

Luke Gallagher

I think toys are important. I need them. They make me happy. I also think you need friends. My best friend's name is Jack.

You probably noticed that some members of the Gallagher family confused needs with wants. It is important to remember that meeting our needs is much more important than getting the things we want.

The connection between human needs and rights

Human needs are the things we need to survive, to thrive as individuals, and to lead happy and healthy lives. When these needs are met, human dignity is respected. There is a close relationship between human needs and rights. Human rights set out our entitlements to many of our most basic needs. When these rights are respected and protected, our human needs can be met.

Let's look at some rights that every child is entitled to. As you read each right, think about the human need(s) connected to that right.

Right 1

You have the right to be alive.

Right 2

You have the right to live with a family who cares for you.

Right 3

You have the right to good-quality education. You should be encouraged to go to school to the highest level you can.

Right 4

You have the right to food, water and clothing.

Right 5

You have the right to a safe place to live.

Right 6

You have the right to meet with friends and join groups.

(Adapted from the United Nations Convention on the Rights of the Child)

? Questions

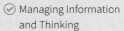

⊘ Being Literate
⊘ Being Numerate
⊘ Managing Information and Thinking
⊘ Staying Well

1 Study the six rights above. Fill in the grid below by stating what need(s) are associated with each right.

Human right	Human need(s)
Right 1	
Right 2	
Right 3	
Right 4	
Right 5	
Right 6	

2 In your own words, briefly describe the relationship between human needs and rights.

Take action!

- ⊘ Being Creative
- ⊘ Being Literate
- ⊘ Communicating
- ⊘ Managing Information and Thinking
- ⊘ Managing Myself
- ⊘ Working with Others

There are many situations where individuals or communities are deprived of their human needs. These include:

- ❯ Famine
- ❯ Drought
- ❯ War
- ❯ Homelessness
- ❯ Poverty
- ❯ Natural disasters.

Choose one of the situations/issues above. Write a report explaining how this situation/issue deprives an individual or community of their needs. Give examples. Name the needs that are not being met. Make reference to how certain human rights are being denied as a result. Refer to the human rights documents in Chapter 7 to help you. When you have completed this action, share your report with the rest of your class.

Don't forget to complete your reflections in your reflective journal.

HUMAN DIGNITY:
THE BASIS FOR HUMAN RIGHTS

Access to food and water: A global challenge

Learning outcomes

By the end of this chapter you will have accessed and interpreted numerical data showing the local and global distribution of basic resources such as food and water. Having interpreted the data, you should be able to identify patterns of inequality.

Key skills you will use in this chapter

- ✓ Being Creative
- ✓ Being Literate
- ✓ Being Numerate
- ✓ Communicating
- ✓ Managing Information and Thinking
- ✓ Managing Myself
- ✓ Staying Well
- ✓ Working with Others

Key words

- Inequalities
- Hunger
- Malnutrition
- Food security
- Poverty
- Weather
- Climate change
- Food waste
- War
- Conflict
- Food poverty
- Sanitation
- Contaminated
- Hygiene
- Analyse
- Data
- Sub-Saharan Africa
- Gender equality issue

Wellbeing indicators in this chapter

In the last chapter you learned about the importance of human needs and how they can help us to lead happy, healthy lives and develop fully as human beings. It is difficult for us to imagine what our lives would be like if we did not have access to our most basic human needs. Unfortunately, this is the daily reality for millions of people throughout the world.

Food and clean water are important resources and are two of our most basic needs. We need them for our survival, health and development. However, huge **inequalities** exist in terms of access to food and clean water.

Challenge ❶ Food inequality

Enough food is produced to feed every person on the planet. However, hundreds of millions of people around the world experience **hunger** and struggle to feed themselves and their families on a daily basis.

Huge inequalities exist in terms of access to food. **Food security** is a term often used to describe the ability of an individual to access nutritious food on a regular basis. The World Food Summit (1996) defines food security as follows:

> *Food security exists when all people, at all times, have physical and economic access to safe and nutritious food that meets their dietary needs and food preferences for an active and healthy life.*

Food insecurity exists when people don't have access to nutritious food on a regular basis. This leads to hunger and **malnutrition**. The infographic below outlines facts and figures about world hunger.

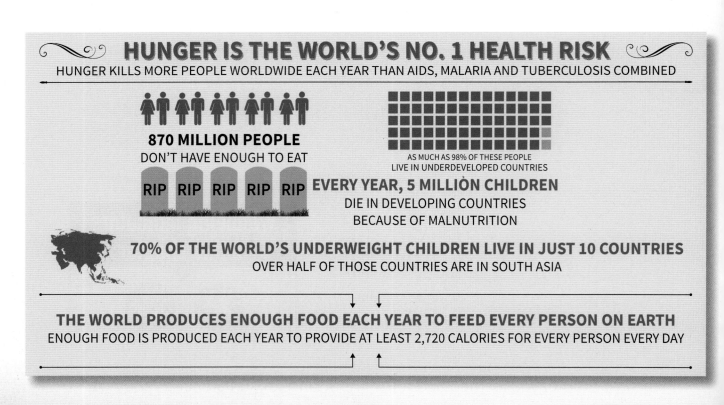

HUNGER IS THE WORLD'S NO. 1 HEALTH RISK
HUNGER KILLS MORE PEOPLE WORLDWIDE EACH YEAR THAN AIDS, MALARIA AND TUBERCULOSIS COMBINED

870 MILLION PEOPLE
DON'T HAVE ENOUGH TO EAT

RIP RIP RIP RIP RIP

AS MUCH AS 98% OF THESE PEOPLE
LIVE IN UNDERDEVELOPED COUNTRIES

EVERY YEAR, 5 MILLION CHILDREN
DIE IN DEVELOPING COUNTRIES
BECAUSE OF MALNUTRITION

70% OF THE WORLD'S UNDERWEIGHT CHILDREN LIVE IN JUST 10 COUNTRIES
OVER HALF OF THOSE COUNTRIES ARE IN SOUTH ASIA

THE WORLD PRODUCES ENOUGH FOOD EACH YEAR TO FEED EVERY PERSON ON EARTH
ENOUGH FOOD IS PRODUCED EACH YEAR TO PROVIDE AT LEAST 2,720 CALORIES FOR EVERY PERSON EVERY DAY

Questions

Having studied the infographic on the previous page, answer the following questions in your copybook.

1   What is the world's number one health risk?

2   How many people don't have enough to eat? Are you surprised by this figure? Why or why not?

3   Name some countries or regions where hunger and malnutrition are major problems.

4   How many children die each year as a result of malnutrition?

5   There is enough food produced every year to provide how many calories to each person?

- ⊘ Being Literate
- ⊘ Being Numerate
- ⊘ Managing Information and Thinking
- ⊘ Managing Myself
- ⊘ Staying Well

Why do world hunger and malnutrition exist?

There are many reasons why hunger and malnutrition are a serious problem in the world today.

 ## Poverty

People living in **poverty** cannot afford nutritious food for themselves or their families. People often go without food, which makes them weak and unable to earn a living. Children living in poverty are often hungry and malnourished and as a result experience stunted growth. This can affect their ability to earn a decent living when they reach adulthood.

In many countries in the developing world, people rely on farming to feed their families and earn a living. Sometimes farmers cannot afford the seeds for their crops. As a result, farmers are unable to feed their families and earn a living. This leads to hunger and malnutrition and pushes families further into poverty.

 ## Weather and climate

Weather events such as tropical storms, flooding and drought are becoming more common. For example, drought is one of the main reasons for food shortages in the world today. In recent times, a lack of rainfall led to the failure of crops and the loss of livestock in countries such as Ethiopia, Kenya and Somalia.

Climate change has also made it difficult to grow crops. Increased temperatures in some areas has negatively affected the quality of the land and has led to soil erosion and desertification, which makes it hard to grow crops and rear livestock.

③ Food waste

Almost one-third of all the food produced in the world is never eaten. **Food waste** is a major issue, particularly in the developed world. Huge inequalities therefore exist between the developed and the developing world. Think about food in your household. Is food thrown out on a regular basis? Considering that millions of people worldwide go to bed hungry each night, do you think that this is fair? What are the things that you and your family could do to prevent food waste?

④ War and conflict

Throughout the world, **war** and **conflict** disrupt farming and food production. War and conflict force millions of families from their homes. In many cases, these people have no way to feed themselves or their families. This creates hunger emergencies in war zones.

Sometimes food is used as a weapon when opponents starve communities into submission. In addition, landmines are often placed on farmland, preventing the farmers from accessing their crops. As a result, many farmers abandon their land, which leaves them without any way to feed their families. In countries such as the Democratic Republic of Congo and Somalia, where war and conflict are common, millions of people go hungry on a daily basis.

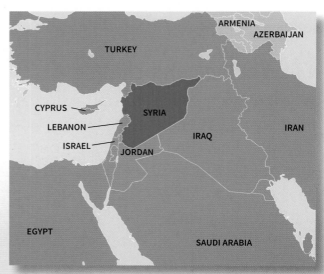

The war in Syria has displaced millions of people. As a result, millions of people have gone hungry and many have died of starvation.

Connect and communicate

There are many organisations at home and around the world that try to tackle hunger and malnutrition in the developing world.

Connect with one such organisation and find out about the ways in which they are trying to eradicate hunger and malnutrition.

- ✓ Being Literate
- ✓ Communicating
- ✓ Managing Information and Thinking
- ✓ Managing Myself
- ✓ Working with Others

Food poverty in Ireland

Hunger and malnutrition are issues we often associate with countries in the developing world. However, these issues also exist in developed countries such as Ireland. Every day in Ireland, thousands of men, women and children experience **food poverty**. Food poverty is the inability to access or afford good, nutritious food on a regular basis.

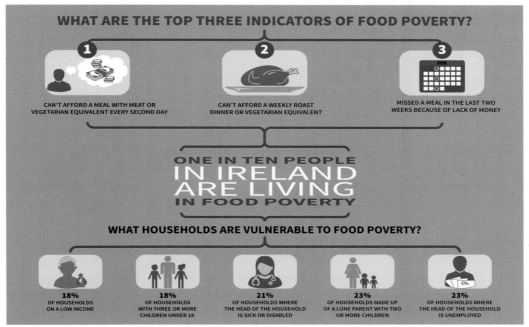

WHAT ARE THE TOP THREE INDICATORS OF FOOD POVERTY?

1. CAN'T AFFORD A MEAL WITH MEAT OR VEGETARIAN EQUIVALENT EVERY SECOND DAY
2. CAN'T AFFORD A WEEKLY ROAST DINNER OR VEGETARIAN EQUIVALENT
3. MISSED A MEAL IN THE LAST TWO WEEKS BECAUSE OF LACK OF MONEY

ONE IN TEN PEOPLE IN IRELAND ARE LIVING IN FOOD POVERTY

WHAT HOUSEHOLDS ARE VULNERABLE TO FOOD POVERTY?

- **18%** OF HOUSEHOLDS ON A LOW INCOME
- **18%** OF HOUSEHOLDS WITH THREE OR MORE CHILDREN UNDER 18
- **21%** OF HOUSEHOLDS WHERE THE HEAD OF THE HOUSEHOLD IS SICK OR DISABLED
- **23%** OF HOUSEHOLDS MADE UP OF A LONE PARENT WITH TWO OR MORE CHILDREN
- **23%** OF HOUSEHOLDS WHERE THE HEAD OF THE HOUSEHOLD IS UNEMPLOYED

Questions

Study the food poverty infographic above and answer the following questions in your copybook.

1. How many people in Ireland are living in food poverty?
2. Name the top three indicators of food poverty.
3. Who is most likely to be affected by food poverty in Ireland?
4. What percentage of households on low incomes experience food poverty?
5. How might food poverty deny an individual their human dignity?

- ✓ Being Literate
- ✓ Being Numerate
- ✓ Managing Information and Thinking
- ✓ Managing Myself
- ✓ Staying Well

Tackling food poverty in Ireland: The work of FoodCloud

In Ireland, thousands of people live in food poverty even though 1 million tonnes of food are thrown out by Irish consumers and businesses every year.

To address this wastage and to reach those experiencing food poverty, two young women set up FoodCloud. FoodCloud encourages businesses such as supermarket chains to prevent food waste by redirecting that food to people who need it the most. FoodCloud has already provided millions of meals to people, ensuring that basic needs are met.

This is how FoodCloud works:

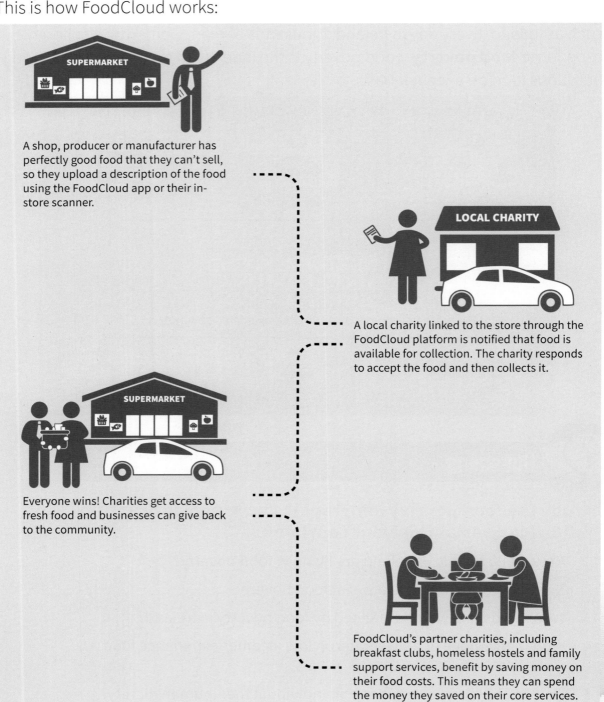

A shop, producer or manufacturer has perfectly good food that they can't sell, so they upload a description of the food using the FoodCloud app or their in-store scanner.

A local charity linked to the store through the FoodCloud platform is notified that food is available for collection. The charity responds to accept the food and then collects it.

Everyone wins! Charities get access to fresh food and businesses can give back to the community.

FoodCloud's partner charities, including breakfast clubs, homeless hostels and family support services, benefit by saving money on their food costs. This means they can spend the money they saved on their core services.

Questions

Examine the infographic on the previous page and answer the following questions in your copybook.

- ☑ Being Literate
- ☑ Managing Information and Thinking
- ☑ Managing Myself

1   How do shops, producers and manufacturers let charities know that food is available for collection?

2   In what ways are businesses giving back to the community?

3   How do partner charities benefit from the work of FoodCloud?

Tackling food poverty abroad

Read the newspaper article below. It outlines the efforts of the French government to end food poverty.

French law forbids food waste from supermarkets

France has become the first country in the world to ban supermarkets from throwing away or destroying unsold food, forcing them instead to donate it to charities and food banks.

Under a law passed unanimously by the French senate, large shops will no longer bin good-quality food approaching its best-before date. Charities will be able to give out millions more free meals each year to people struggling to afford to eat.

The law follows a grassroots campaign in France by shoppers, anti-poverty campaigners and those opposed to food waste. The campaign, which led to a petition, was started by the councillor Arash Derambarsh. In December a bill on the issue passed through the National Assembly, having been introduced by the former food industry minister Guillaume Garot.

Campaigners now hope to persuade the EU to adopt similar legislation across member states.

Source: The Guardian, 4 February 2016

 ## Take action!

- ☑ Being Creative
- ☑ Being Literate
- ☑ Communicating
- ☑ Managing Information and Thinking
- ☑ Managing Myself

Having read the newspaper report above, do you think this law is a good idea? Do you think a similar law should be introduced in Ireland?

Write a letter or email you could send to your local TD calling for a similar law to be introduced in Ireland. Your letter or email should include a convincing argument for why such a law should be introduced.

Challenge ❷ Water

Access to clean drinking water is a vital human need and human right. Although many of us take clean drinking water for granted, there are millions of people across the globe for whom clean drinking water is not a reality. In some countries, rural areas in particular have no piped water or **sanitation**. Many people rely on rivers, sinkholes and wells for their water. Because so many people use these sources, they can become **contaminated** very easily and the water becomes unsafe to drink. As a result, people often have to walk many miles in search of a clean water source.

Although there have been huge improvements in the provision of clean water, it still remains one of the biggest global challenges.

Why is clean water important?

❶ Unsafe drinking water is the biggest cause of sickness and death in the world

🌐 More than 3.4 million people die from water, sanitation and **hygiene** issues every year.

🌐 Unsafe water kills 200 children every hour. The diseases these children die from are preventable.

🌐 A child dies every 21 seconds from diarrhoea.

🌐 Half of all the world's hospital beds are filled with people suffering from a water-related disease.

② Water has a big impact on people's lives

Both women and children spend many hours every day searching for clean water. This means:

🌐 Millions of children (girls in particular) spend much of their day searching for clean water. As a result, children don't go to school, which denies them the right to an education.

🌐 It is estimated that in just one day, 200 million hours are spent by women and girls collecting water for their families.

🌐 Without clean water, it is difficult to address global problems such as poverty, hunger and AIDS.

③ Lack of clean water affects millions of people worldwide

🌐 780 million people worldwide don't have access to clean water.

🌐 One-third of the world's population lacks adequate sanitation.

Where are the problems?

Huge inequalities exist in terms of access to clean water. Access to clean water is a major problem in parts of Africa and Asia. The infographic on the next page shows the locations of countries that have difficulty locating a clean water source.

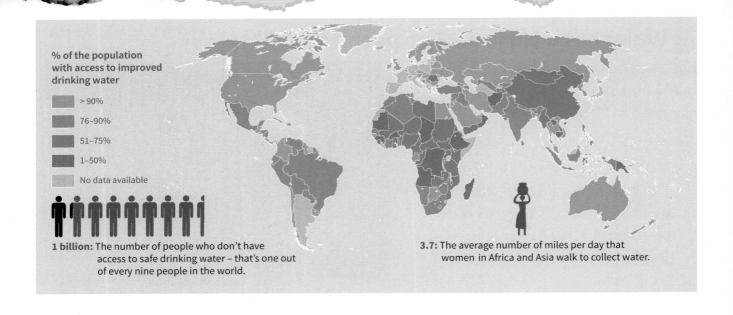

% of the population with access to improved drinking water

> 90%
76–90%
51–75%
1–50%
No data available

1 billion: The number of people who don't have access to safe drinking water – that's one out of every nine people in the world.

3.7: The average number of miles per day that women in Africa and Asia walk to collect water.

? ... Questions

- ✓ Being Literate
- ✓ Being Numerate
- ✓ Managing Information and Thinking
- ✓ Staying Well

Study the map above and analyse the data, then answer the following questions in your copybook.

1   List five countries where access to clean water is an issue. Name the relevant continents. Use your atlas to help you.

2   What is the average distance that women in Africa and Asia walk each day in order to access clean water?

3   Why, do you think, do some people in Africa and Asia not have access to clean water?

Wells or clean water sources can sometimes be located many miles from where people live. In some regions, especially in **sub-Saharan Africa**, many people spend more than an hour on each trip to collect water. Inequalities exist in terms of who collects water. It is usually collected by women and young girls. Many have to travel with heavy drums or containers filled with water so that their families can drink, eat and stay healthy.

Collecting water is a **gender equality issue**. The graph on the next page shows who has responsibility for collecting water in rural areas. It shows the hours per day women and girls and men and boys spend collecting water.

Who collects water in rural areas around the world?

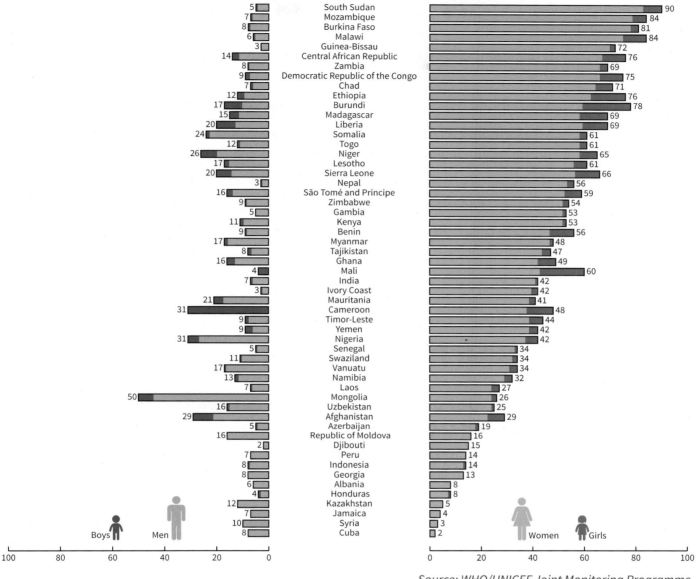

Source: WHO/UNICEF Joint Monitoring Programme

Imagine!

Imagine that you are writing a report for your school newsletter to highlight gender inequality in terms of water collection.

Write down four key findings from the data (information) given in the chart above that you could use in your report.

- ⊘ Being Creative
- ⊘ Being Literate
- ⊘ Communicating
- ⊘ Managing Information and Thinking
- ⊘ Managing Myself

Connect and communicate

- Being Literate
- Communicating
- Managing Information and Thinking
- Managing Myself
- Working with Others

Connect and communicate with an organisation that tackles the global water crisis. Communicate by email, social media, letter or phone.

Find out about projects that the organisation has undertaken and how you can play a role in providing clean water for everyone. Here are some useful organisations to help you to get started:

- Billion Bottle Project
- Blue Planet Network
- One Drop
- WaterAid
- Water to Thrive
- World Water Relief

 **Video** WaterAid

 # Take action!

- Being Creative
- Being Literate
- Being Numerate
- Communicating
- Managing Information and Thinking
- Managing Myself

Create your own infographic about unequal access to clean water and sanitation.

Use data from the textbook or source your own data online. Create your infographic in your reflective journal.

 Don't forget to complete your reflections in your reflective journal.

Human rights timeline

Learning outcomes

By the end of this chapter you will be able to create a timeline tracing the origin of human rights, showing five or more key dates, events, people and documents.

Key words

- Charter
- Declaration
- Convention

Key skills you will use in this chapter

- ✓ Being Creative
- ✓ Being Literate
- ✓ Being Numerate
- ✓ Communicating
- ✓ Managing Information and Thinking
- ✓ Managing Myself
- ✓ Staying Well
- ✓ Working with Others

Wellbeing indicators in this chapter

Human rights timeline

An interest in human rights can be traced back as far as early civilisation. Let's examine some key dates, events and documents that have shaped human rights.

The road to human rights

539 BC: Cyrus the Great
The first emperor of Persia, Cyrus the Great, conquered the city of Babylon. He freed the slaves, gave people the right to choose their own religion and established racial equality. A record of these rights and freedoms was carved on a clay cylinder, which is now referred to as the Cyrus Cylinder. Many historians believe that this was the first **charter** of human rights.

Seventh century: Brehon law
Brehon law was written by wandering lawyers called Brehons (male and female). No police force or prison was necessary. Many historians believe that Brehon law was ahead of its time because it promoted equal rights for men and women and prioritised environmental protection.

1789: The Declaration of the Rights of Man
The French National Assembly passed the Declaration of the Rights of Man and the Citizen. Th[e] document declared that a[ll] men (citizens) 'are born fr[ee] and remain free and equa[l in] rights'. The **declaration** a[lso] promoted freedom of spe[ech] and thought.

1000

500 AD

500 BC

1 AD

1500

1600

1700

From 500 BC
The Ancient Greeks used the words *isegoria* (freedom of speech) and *isonomia* (equality before the law) for the first time.

1215: The Magna Carta
King John of England reluctantly signed the Magna Carta, which stated that the king was not above the law. The document gave rights to 'freemen' in England. This document ensured that all freemen were entitled to a fair trial.

1689: The British Bill of Rights
The British Bill of Rights was a law that guaranteed free elections in England. It also encouraged freedom of speech and ensured that citizens didn't have to pay huge fines or suffer cruel punishments.

1776: The American Declaration of Independence
The American Declaration of Independence proclaimed that all men are created equal and are entitled to the rights listed.

1865: Slavery is abolished in the US

In 1865 the US House of Representatives passed the 13th Amendment to the US Constitution, which abolished slavery in America. Abraham Lincoln and Frederick Douglass, among others, had campaigned for years against slavery. The amendment reads, 'Neither slavery nor involuntary servitude…shall exist in the United States, or any place subject to their jurisdiction.'

1945: The United Nations is established

The United Nations was founded to advance peace between countries. One of the main aims of the United Nations is to foster 'respect for human rights and fundamental freedoms for all without distinction as to race, sex, language or religion'.

1950: The European Convention on Human Rights

The Council of Europe drafted the European Convention on Human Rights. The **convention** protects the rights of people living and working in Europe. The convention also outlines the role of the state in the protection of human rights.

1994: South Africa holds its first free democratic elections

After apartheid was abolished, South Africa held its first free democratic elections, in which citizens of all races were allowed to vote. Millions queued in lines to cast their vote. The new National Assembly elected Nelson Mandela as the president.

1800 — 1900 — 1950 — 2000 — 2020

1961: Amnesty International founded

Amnesty International was founded. It is an organisation that promotes human rights and raises awareness about human rights abuses throughout the world.

1789: The US Bill of Rights

The first ten amendments to the US Constitution make up the Bill of Rights. This bill defends civil liberties such as freedom of speech, freedom of religion, freedom of assembly and the entitlement to petition the government to correct wrongs.

1893: Women's right to vote

New Zealand became the first country in the world to grant women the right to vote. This happened as a result of numerous campaigns by women in New Zealand who highlighted this serious inequality between women and men.

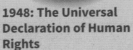

1948: The Universal Declaration of Human Rights

The Universal Declaration of Human Rights was adopted by the United Nations on 10 December 1948. This declaration set down the rights to which everyone is entitled.

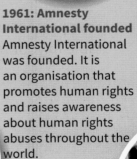

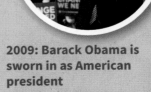

2009: Barack Obama is sworn in as American president

Barack Obama was sworn in as the 44th President of the United States. He became America's first black president.

? ... Questions

1 Which six human rights documents or events outlined on the previous pages do you think were the most important? Give a reason why you chose each one.

2 Choose one of these documents or events and explain how it helped to promote or protect human rights.

- ⊘ Being Creative
- ⊘ Being Literate
- ⊘ Being Numerate
- ⊘ Managing Information and Thinking
- ⊘ Managing Myself
- ⊘ Staying Well

Take action!

- ⊘ Being Creative
- ⊘ Being Literate
- ⊘ Being Numerate
- ⊘ Managing Information and Thinking
- ⊘ Managing Myself

Create a timeline, illustration or story about the evolution of human rights. You may refer to some of the human rights events already mentioned. However, try to include at least five other human rights events. These could include:

❯ Key human rights documents

❯ An event that promoted human rights

❯ A law that protected human rights

❯ A speech or action that defended the rights of others

❯ The work of an individual or an organisation in protecting human rights.

Your presentation can be in an audio, visual or digital format. Use the table in your reflective journal to help you.

Don't forget to complete your reflections in your reflective journal.

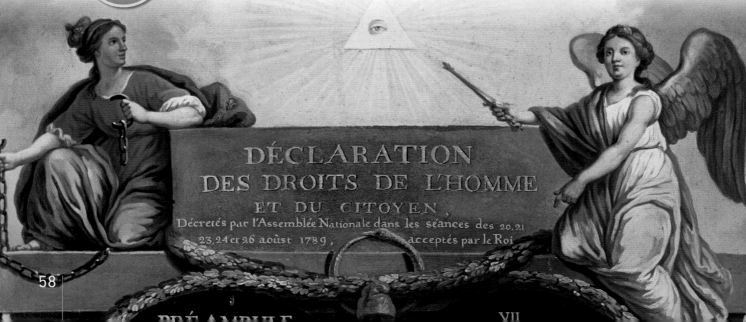

Chapter 6

UNIT 2

HUMAN RIGHTS INSTRUMENTS

Human rights champions

Learning outcomes

By the end of this chapter you will be able to share stories of inspirational individuals or groups who have worked for the protection and promotion of human rights in Ireland and throughout the world.

Key words

- 🔑 Human rights activists
- 🔑 Boycott
- 🔑 Segregation
- 🔑 Campaigner
- 🔑 Apartheid

Key skills you will use in this chapter

- ✓ Being Creative
- ✓ Being Literate
- ✓ Being Numerate
- ✓ Communicating
- ✓ Managing Information and Thinking
- ✓ Managing Myself
- ✓ Staying Well
- ✓ Working with Others

Wellbeing indicators in this chapter

Human rights champions

Throughout history, many people have stood up for the rights of others. Sometimes risking their own lives, these people have inspired others to speak out and stand up for the rights of others too. These human rights champions are also known as **human rights activists** because they took responsibility for protecting and promoting their rights or the rights of others.

Human rights champions from history

Frederick Douglass (1818–1895)

Frederick Douglass was a public speaker, writer, human rights leader and anti-slavery **campaigner** in the nineteenth century. Born into slavery, Douglass experienced first-hand the injustices endured by the many slaves working on plantations and in domestic service in America. After he escaped slavery when he was twenty years old, he campaigned against slavery and social injustices in the world. He even visited Ireland and met Daniel O'Connell. He was also a champion of women's rights. Douglass went on to become the first African-American to be elected to high office in the US government.

Irena Sendler (1910–2008)

Irena Sendler was a Polish nurse and social worker who worked in the Polish underground movement during the Second World War. During the war, Jewish people were rounded up by the Nazis and placed in ghettos, which they were not allowed to leave. The people who lived in the ghettos were later transported to concentration camps. During this time, Sendler worked for the Department of Social Welfare. As part of her job, she often visited the Warsaw ghetto in Poland. When she saw the conditions and the injustice experienced by the Jewish people, she tried to help them. Sendler helped to smuggle babies and young children out of the ghetto so that they could have a future. She did so by any means possible: in toolboxes, sacks, suitcases and even coffins. It is estimated that she saved the lives of over 2,500 Jewish children. The Gestapo found out about Sendler's work and she was arrested in 1943, imprisoned and tortured. Despite this, she would not give up the names of the people who helped her. Sendler escaped prison and went on the run until the end of the Second World War. If you look online, you can find clips of Irena Sendler, describing her actions.

Rosa Parks (1913–2005)

1n 1955, Rosa Parks boarded a bus in Montgomery, Alabama, in the United States. Not long into her journey, she was asked to give up her seat to a white man. She refused. At that time, there were laws in some US states that segregated white and black people in schools, shops, restaurants and public transport. Parks's refusal to give up her seat meant she was arrested. As a result, she lost her job. In response, many black people boycotted public transport. This became known as the Montgomery Bus Boycott. A **boycott** is a form of protest where people refuse to use a service or buy a product. Parks's actions sparked a non-violent black civil rights movement in the United States. This movement, led by Martin Luther King, called for the end of racial **segregation** in the United States. Rosa Parks is still referred to today as the first lady of civil rights.

Willie Bermingham (1942–1990)

Willie Bermingham was a member of the Dublin Fire Brigade in the 1970s. During the course of his work, he found the body of an elderly man in a filthy flat. His body had been lying there for weeks. Bermingham was shocked by this discovery. He soon realised that many old people were living in dreadful conditions without fuel or food. He also realised that many of Dublin's elderly were lonely and alone. Some were forgotten by their families. Others were too unwell to leave their homes and so became isolated. Willie Bermingham set up ALONE (A Little Offering Never Ends) in 1977. The aim of the organisation is to help older people in need. This organisation provides food, clothing and fuel to those who most need it. It also provides accommodation for elderly people who find themselves alone and isolated. ALONE campaigns for the rights of older people in Ireland. Willie Bermingham died in 1990, but his legacy lives on.

 Research

- ✓ Being Literate
- ✓ Communicating
- ✓ Managing Information and Thinking
- ✓ Managing Myself

Go online to find out more about the work of ALONE in its efforts to protect the rights of older people.

Human rights champions today

Malala Yousafzai

Malala Yousafzai was born in Pakistan in 1997. When Malala was a young child, the Taliban was trying to seize power in Pakistan. The Taliban believed that girls should not receive an education. They started attacking schools. Many parents lived in fear of the Taliban and did not send their daughters to school.

In 2009, Malala began secretly blogging for the BBC, speaking out against the Taliban. She spoke about the right of girls to an education. The Taliban heard about this and issued death threats against her. Despite this, Malala continued to go to school. In 2012, she was shot by a masked gunman on her way home from school. She remained in a critical condition in hospital for many months. Fortunately, Malala made a full recovery. She continues to defend human rights. In 2015, seventeen-year-old Malala became the youngest person ever to receive the Nobel Peace Prize.

Mary Manning and the Dunnes Stores strikers

Mary Manning had heard about the system of **apartheid** in South Africa. It was a system that deprived black people of their human rights. In 1984, she was working on the checkouts at Dunnes Stores in Henry Street, Dublin. Manning refused to put a sale of South African fruit through the cash register. She believed that by doing this she would be sending the South African government a message against apartheid. Manning was suspended from work. Ten of her co-workers went on strike to support her. The strike raised huge awareness about apartheid. The strikers were determined to stand up for what was right. Dunnes Stores refused to change their policy. The strike finally ended in 1987 when the Irish government brought in a ban on South African goods. On his visit to Dublin in 1990, Nelson Mandela thanked the strikers for standing up for the rights of black South Africans. In honour of her activism, Mary Manning has a street named after her in Johannesburg, South Africa.

Fr Peter McVerry

Fr Peter McVerry began working in Dublin's inner city in 1974. In the course of his work, he was shocked to discover a large number of homeless young men living on the streets. He felt the need to do something about this. He opened a hostel for them, which was a great success. McVerry later founded the Peter McVerry Trust, an organisation that provides a range of services for homeless people. As well as providing accommodation, this trust also offers educational courses and detox centres for its service users. Peter McVerry has tirelessly campaigned for the rights of the homeless and has won many awards for his efforts.

Christina Noble

Christina Noble was born in Dublin in the 1940s. When her mother died, Christina and her brothers and sisters were put into different orphanages. Noble escaped her orphanage and once slept in a hole she had dug for herself in the Phoenix Park. When she was eighteen, she moved to England. While she was there she had a dream that she would help children living in poverty. Years later, that dream brought her to Vietnam. On Noble's first visit, she saw thousands of children living in extreme poverty, with many of them living on the streets. Noble knew she had to help them. She set up the Christina Noble Children's Foundation, a voluntary organisation that provides food, medical care, education and shelter for poor children and their families. This foundation also helps to protect children from exploitation. Noble has expanded the charity's work into Mongolia.

Research

✓ Being Literate
✓ Communicating
✓ Managing Information and Thinking
✓ Managing Myself

Find out more about the work of the Christina Noble Children's Foundation by visiting its website.

Take action!

✓ Being Creative
✓ Managing Information and Thinking
✓ Being Literate
✓ Communicating
✓ Managing Information and Thinking
✓ Managing Myself

Having learned about some human rights champions past and present, select the one who inspires you the most and who you think should be given the title 'Human Rights Champion of All Time'.

Do further research on the life and work of this person. Record your findings in your reflective journal. If you wish, you can make a presentation to the class. Your presentation can be in audio, visual or digital format.

Human rights organisations

Video Amnesty International

Amnesty International

Amnesty International is a worldwide organisation that campaigns for human rights. It was founded in 1961 by a British lawyer,
Peter Benenson. Benenson wrote a letter defending two Portuguese students who were imprisoned simply because they had raised their glasses in a toast to freedom. Benenson realised the power of the pen and encouraged others to write letters on the prisoners' behalf. Thousands of letters were written, which put pressure on the Portuguese president to release the two prisoners. This letter-writing campaign was responsible for the eventual release of the prisoners.

Since 1961, Amnesty International has grown into a worldwide organisation with nearly 2 million members. Amnesty encourages its members to highlight human rights abuses around the globe through letter-writing campaigns, petitions, fundraising drives and protests.

Amnesty campaigns for an end to human rights abuses such as:

- 🌐 The death penalty
- 🌐 Violence against women
- 🌐 Human trafficking
- 🌐 Prisoners of conscience
- 🌐 Child labour
- 🌐 Torture
- 🌐 Racism
- 🌐 Abuses against refugees.

 ## Connect and communicate

Connect with Amnesty International Ireland online or in person. Find out about some of its campaigns and how you can play a role in ending human rights abuses.

- ⊘ Being Literate
- ⊘ Communicating
- ⊘ Managing Information and Thinking
- ⊘ Managing Myself
- ⊘ Staying Well
- ⊘ Working with Others

Irish Human Rights and Equality Commission (IHREC)

The Irish Human Rights and Equality Commission was set up to promote equality and protect human rights in Ireland. It is an independent public body that works with the government to ensure that laws and government policy in Ireland protect human rights. This organisation also gives advice and information to members of the public whose human rights have been infringed.

Human Rights Watch

Human Rights Watch (HRW) is a non-governmental organisation that promotes human rights internationally. HRW produces research reports about human rights abuses worldwide. This organisation uses these reports to highlight human rights abuses and to put pressure on governments to change policy so that human rights are respected and promoted.

Imagine!

- ⊘ Being Creative
- ⊘ Being Literate
- ⊘ Managing Information and Thinking
- ⊘ Managing Myself
- ⊘ Staying Well

Think about a human rights issue you feel strongly about. Imagine that you have been given a large sum of money to set up your own human rights organisation. Your organisation aims to promote, protect or campaign for this right.

1 Name the human right that your organisation is protecting or promoting.

2 Give a name to your human rights organisation.

3 Briefly describe a campaign that your organisation could undertake to protect human rights.

Take action!

- ⊘ Communicating
- ⊘ Managing Information and Thinking
- ⊘ Managing Myself
- ⊘ Working with Others

Invite a member of a human rights organisation to make a presentation about their work to students in your school.

Don't forget to complete your reflections in your reflective journal.

Human rights instruments

Learning outcomes

By the end of this chapter you will be able to communicate your understanding of how the Universal Declaration of Human Rights, the United Nations Convention on the Rights of the Child and the European Convention on Human Rights apply to your life in terms of your rights and responsibilities.

Key skills you will use in this chapter

- ✓ **Being Creative**
- ✓ **Being Literate**
- ✓ **Being Numerate**
- ✓ **Communicating**
- ✓ **Managing Information and Thinking**
- ✓ **Managing Myself**
- ✓ **Staying Well**
- ✓ **Working with Others**

Key words

- Human rights instruments
- International
- Regional
- Declaration
- Convention
- United Nations
- Universal Declaration of Human Rights
- European Convention on Human Rights
- UN Convention on the Rights of the Child
- Ratified
- Survival
- Develop
- Participation
- Protection

Wellbeing indicators in this chapter

Human rights instruments

In Chapter 5 you learned about the history of human rights. You might have noticed that the timeline referred to agreements such as conventions, declarations, treaties and bills of rights. These are examples of **human rights instruments**. Human rights instruments are documents that seek to promote and protect human rights.

Human rights instruments can be **international** or **regional**.

🌐 International human rights instruments are the documents that seek to protect the rights of all people across the globe.

🌐 Regional human rights instruments, on the other hand, apply only to people living in certain regions in the world.

There are two main types of human rights instrument:

🌐 A **declaration** is a formal statement. It is not legally binding.

🌐 A **convention** is a legally binding agreement that sets out the rights to which people are entitled.

When governments sign up to human rights instruments, they promise to recognise and safeguard the rights contained in them. In the case of a convention, governments make laws to ensure that human rights are respected and protected.

Document ❶ The Universal Declaration of Human Rights (UDHR)

When the Second World War ended in 1945, people were shocked by the horror and destruction it caused. Over 55 million people had been killed.

Soon after the end of the Second World War, the **United Nations** was set up to keep peace and to solve international problems.

To promote and protect the rights of every person, the United Nations wrote down all the rights to which every human being is entitled. This became known as the **Universal Declaration of Human Rights**. These rights are universal, which means they apply to everyone, regardless of factors such as race, gender, age, religion and social class. The UDHR is an example of an international human rights instrument.

Eleanor Roosevelt was one of the driving forces behind the UDHR. She was chairperson of the UN Human Rights Commission from 1945 to 1951 and US representative at the General Assembly from 1946 to 1952.

Eleanor Roosevelt

THE UNIVERSAL DECLARATION OF
HUMAN RIGHTS

**The UDHR was accepted by the United Nations General Assembly in 1948.
It states the basic rights and fundamental freedoms to which everyone is entitled.**

YOU HAVE THE RESPONSIBILITY TO RESPECT THE RIGHTS OF OTHERS.

WE ARE ALL BORN FREE AND EQUAL.
EVERYONE IS ENTITLED TO THESE RIGHTS NO MATTER WHAT YOUR RACE, RELIGION OR NATIONALITY IS.
EVERYONE HAS THE RIGHT TO LIFE, FREEDOM AND SAFETY.

NO ONE CAN TAKE AWAY ANY OF YOUR RIGHTS.

 No one has the right to hold you in slavery.

 You can travel wherever you want.

 You have the right to social security and are entitled to economic, social and cultural help from your government.

 No one has the right to torture you.

 You have the right to seek asylum in another country if you are being persecuted in your own country.

 You have the right to recognition everywhere as a person before the law.

 Everyone has the right to a nationality.

 Every adult has the right to a job, a fair wage and to join a trade union.

 We are all equal before the law and are entitled to equal protection of the law.

 All adults have the right to marry and to raise a family.

 You have the right to leisure and rest from work.

 You have the right to seek legal help if your rights are violated.

 You have the right to own property.

 Everyone has the right to an adequate standard of living for themselves and their family.

 No one has the right to wrongly imprison you or force you to leave your country.

 Everyone has the right to belong to a religion.

 You have the right to a fair and public trial.

 You have the right to free thought and to voice your opinions to others (freedom of expression).

 Everyone has the right to education.

 Everyone is innocent until proven guilty.

 Everyone has the right to gather as a peaceful assembly.

 Your intellectual property as an artist or scientist should be protected.

You have the right to privacy. No one can interfere with your reputation, family, home or correspondence.

You have the right to help choose government representatives and to take part in governing your country, directly or through chosen representatives.

 We are all entitled to social order so that we can enjoy these rights.

Source: Universal Declaration of Human Rights

Group activity

- Being Creative
- Being Literate
- Communicating
- Managing Information and Thinking
- Managing Myself
- Working with Others

Study the UDHR on the previous page. What rights do you feel are the most important?

- As a group, discuss these rights and choose the five rights that you feel are the most important. Discuss the ways in which these rights apply to your lives.

- Now rank these rights in order of importance, with 1 being the most important. Use the table in your reflective journal. Compare your group's ranking ladder with other groups in the class.

Document ❷ The European Convention on Human Rights (ECHR)

The **European Convention on Human Rights** is an example of a regional human rights instrument because it applies only to people living or working in Europe. Drafted in 1950 by the newly established Council of Europe, this convention came into force in 1953. This human rights document also outlines the responsibilities of governments in protecting human rights. This convention is legally binding. As a result, the European Court of Human Rights was set up to protect the rights and freedoms contained in this convention. Individuals who feel that their rights have been denied by their government can take their case to this court. This convention protects the rights of Irish citizens, as it became a part of Irish law in 2003.

Questions

- Being Literate
- Managing Information and Thinking
- Managing Myself

Study the UDHR on page 69 and the ECHR on page 71.

1   Describe some ways in which these documents are similar.

2   Describe some ways in which these documents are different.

EUROPEAN CONVENTION ON HUMAN RIGHTS

SECTION I: RIGHTS AND FREEDOMS

Article 1: Obligation to respect human rights

If you live in a country that has agreed to this convention, you have a right to these basic rights, whether you are a citizen or not.

Article 2: Right to life

You have the right to life. This right is protected by law.

Article 3: Freedom from torture

Nobody is allowed to torture, harm or humiliate you.

Article 4: Freedom from slavery and forced labour

Nobody is allowed to treat you as a slave and you should not make anyone your slave. No one can force you to work.

Article 5: Right to liberty and security

You have the right to freedom and safety. No one is allowed to take away this right except by legal means. If you are arrested, you have many rights, including the right to understand why you are being arrested, to have a prompt hearing and to challenge your arrest.

Article 6: Right to a fair trial

If you are accused of a crime, you have the right to a fair and public hearing.

Article 7: No punishment without law

You cannot be punished for doing something that was not considered a crime at the time you did it.

Article 8: Right to respect for private and family life, home and correspondence

You have the right to be protected if someone tries to enter your house, open your post or bother you or your family without good reasons.

Article 9: Freedom of thought, conscience and religion

You have the right to your own thoughts and to believe in any religion. You are free to practise your religion or beliefs and also to change them.

Article 10: Freedom of expression

You have the right to think what you want and to responsibly say what you like. You should be able to share your ideas and opinions in any way, including in newspapers and magazines and on the radio, television and internet.

Article 11: Freedom of assembly and association

You have the right to meet peacefully with other people, including the right to form and to join trade unions.

Article 12: Right to marry

When you are legally old enough, you have the right to marry and to have a family.

Article 13: Right to an effective remedy

If your rights are violated by another person or by the government, you have the right to ask for help from the courts or other public bodies to uphold your rights.

Article 14: Freedom from discrimination

You have all the rights and freedoms in this convention regardless of your gender, race, colour, language, religion, political or other opinion, national or social background, association with a minority group, economic status, birth or other status.

Article 15: Exemptions in time of emergency

The government may suspend its duties to uphold these rights and freedoms in times of war. However, this may not include Article 2, the right to life.

Article 16: Restrictions on political activity of aliens

The government cannot restrict your political activity simply because you are not a citizen of that country.

Article 17: Prohibition of abuse of rights

No person, group or government anywhere in the world may do anything to destroy these rights.

Article 18: Limitation on use of restrictions on rights

Your rights and freedoms can only be limited in ways set out in this convention.

SECTION II: EUROPEAN COURT OF HUMAN RIGHTS

Articles 19–51: The European Court of Human Rights

This convention established the European Court of Human Rights. The judges are independent and are elected by the Parliamentary Assembly of the Council of Europe.

SECTION III: MISCELLANEOUS

Articles 52–59: Applying the rights in this convention

The Committee of Ministers of the Council of Europe oversees how governments respect this convention and fulfil their obligations to promote and protect human rights.

Source: Council of Europe

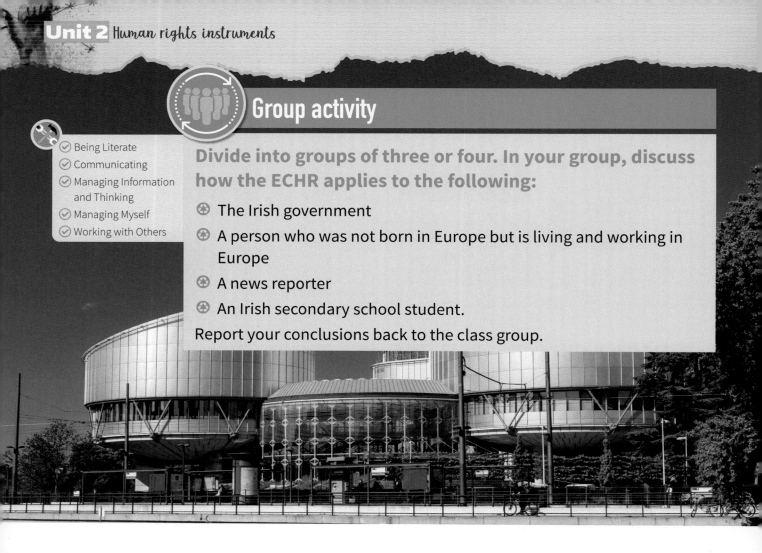

Group activity

- Being Literate
- Communicating
- Managing Information and Thinking
- Managing Myself
- Working with Others

Divide into groups of three or four. In your group, discuss how the ECHR applies to the following:

- ⊕ The Irish government
- ⊕ A person who was not born in Europe but is living and working in Europe
- ⊕ A news reporter
- ⊕ An Irish secondary school student.

Report your conclusions back to the class group.

Document ❸ The UN Convention on the Rights of the Child (UNCRC)

Every child needs special care and protection. Children are among the most vulnerable in society. Throughout the world, many children are denied their rights. In Chapter 4, you learned that millions of children are deprived of the right to an education, for example. To protect the rights of children, the United Nations adopted the **Convention on the Rights of the Child** in 1989. The convention applies to every child under the age of eighteen and sets out the rights to which each child is entitled. A convention is protected by law. Ireland **ratified** this convention in 1990. This means that the Irish government recognises the rights in the UNCRC.

The UNCRC consists of fifty-four articles, which can be broadly divided into the following categories.

Survival rights

Every child has the right to **survival**. Therefore, every child is entitled to access basic needs such as food, water, shelter, medical care and an adequate standard of living.

Development rights

Every child should be given the opportunity to **develop** to reach their potential. To do so, children need education, rest and play. Children should have access to leisure and cultural activities and should be able to access information.

Participation rights

All children have the right to become actively involved in the communities, societies and nations to which they belong. **Participation** rights mean that each child has a voice and can express their opinions on issues that affect them.

Protection rights

Protection rights safeguard every child from abuse, exploitation, torture, cruelty and neglect.

UN CONVENTION ON THE RIGHTS OF THE CHILD

Rights are things that every child should have or be able to do. All children have the same rights. These rights are listed in the UN Convention on the Rights of the Child. Almost every country has agreed to these rights. All the rights are connected to each other and all are equally important. Sometimes we have to think about the rights in terms of what is best for children in a situation and what is critical to life and protection from harm. As you grow, you have more responsibility to make choices and exercise your rights.

Article 1
Everyone under 18 has these rights.

Article 2
All children have these rights, no matter who they are, where they live, what their parents do, what language they speak, what their religion is, whether they are a boy or girl, what their culture is, whether they have a disability, whether they are rich or poor. No child should be treated unfairly on any basis.

Article 3
All adults should do what is best for you. When adults make decisions, they should think about how their decisions will affect children.

Article 4
The government has a responsibility to make sure your rights are protected. They must help your family to protect your rights and create an environment where you can grow and reach your potential.

Article 5
Your family has the responsibility to help you to learn to exercise your rights and to ensure that your rights are protected.

Article 6
You have the right to be alive.

Article 7
You have the right to a name and this should be officially recognised by the government. You have the right to a nationality (to belong to a country).

Article 8
You have the right to an identity – an official record of who you are. No one should take this away from you.

Article 9
You have the right to live with your parent(s), unless it is bad for you. You have the right to live with a family who cares for you.

Article 10
If you live in a different country from your parents, you have the right to be together in the same place.

Article 11
You have the right to be protected from kidnapping.

Article 12
You have the right to give your opinion and for adults to listen and take it seriously.

Article 13
You have the right to find out things and share what you think with others by talking, drawing, writing or in any other way unless it harms or offends other people.

Article 14
You have the right to choose your own religion and beliefs. Your parents should help you to decide what is right and wrong and what is best for you.

Article 15
You have the right to choose your own friends and join or set up groups, as long as it isn't harmful to others.

Article 16
You have the right to privacy.

Article 17
You have the right to get information that is important to your wellbeing from radio, newspapers, books, computers and other sources. Adults should make sure that the information you are getting isn't harmful and help you to find and understand the information you need.

Article 18
You have the right to be raised by your parent(s) if possible.

Article 19
You have the right to be protected from being hurt and mistreated, in body or mind.

Article 20
You have the right to special care and help if you can't live with your parents.

Article 21
You have the right to care and protection if you are adopted or in foster care.

Article 22
You have the right to special protection and help if you are a refugee, as well as all the rights in this convention.

Article 23
You have the right to special education and care if you have a disability, as well as all the rights in this convention, so that you can live a full life.

Article 24
You have the right to the best healthcare possible, safe water to drink, nutritious food, a clean and safe environment and information to help you stay well.

Article 25
If you live in care or in other situations away from home, you have the right to have these living arrangements looked at regularly to see if they are the most appropriate.

Article 26
You have the right to help from the government if you are poor or in need.

Article 27
You have the right to food, clothing, a safe place to live and to have your basic needs met. You should not be disadvantaged so that you can't do many of the things other kids can do.

Article 28
You have the right to a good-quality education. You should be encouraged to go to school to the highest level you can.

Article 29
Your education should help you to use and develop your talents and abilities. It should also help you to learn to live peacefully, protect the environment and respect other people.

Article 30
You have the right to practise your own culture, language and religion – or any you choose. Minority and indigenous groups need special protection of this right.

Article 31
You have the right to play and rest.

Article 32
You have the right to protection from work that harms you and is bad for your health and education. If you work, you have the right to be safe and paid fairly.

Article 33
You have the right to protection from harmful drugs and from the drug trade.

Article 34
You have the right to be free from sexual abuse.

Article 35
No one is allowed to kidnap or sell you.

Article 36
You have the right to protection from any kind of exploitation (being taken advantage of).

Article 37
No one is allowed to punish you in a cruel or harmful way.

Article 38
You have the right to protection and freedom from war. Children under 15 can't be forced to go into the army or take part in war.

Article 39
You have the right to help if you've been hurt, neglected or badly treated.

Article 40
You have the right to legal help and fair treatment in the justice system that respects your rights.

Article 41
If the laws of your country provide better protection of your rights than the articles in this convention, those laws should apply.

Article 42
You have the right to know your rights! Adults should know about these rights and help you to learn about them too.

Articles 43–54
These articles explain how governments and international organisations like UNICEF will work to ensure that children are protected with their rights.

Source: UNICEF

Questions

Study the articles outlined in the UN Convention on the Rights of the Child on the opposite page. Answer the questions that follow.

✓ Being Literate
✓ Communicating
✓ Managing Information and Thinking
✓ Managing Myself
✓ Staying Well

1   Copy the table into your copybook and write down three articles that refer to each of the four categories.

Survival rights	Development rights	Participation rights	Protection rights

2   In 1990, the Irish government ratified the Convention on the Rights of the Child. List five responsibilities that the Irish government has towards children living in Ireland today.

3   Go online to find out about one organisation in Ireland that promotes and protects the rights of children.

Take action!

Your class would like to raise awareness about children's rights in your school. In your copybook, describe one action your class could undertake to raise awareness about children's rights in your school, then describe the action.

✓ Being Creative
✓ Being Literate
✓ Communicating
✓ Managing Information and Thinking
✓ Managing Myself
✓ Staying Well
✓ Working with Others

Don't forget to complete your reflections in your reflective journal.

Chapter 8

Classification of human rights

Learning outcomes

By the end of this chapter you should be able to identify examples of social, economic, cultural, language, civic, religious, political and environmental rights.

Key words

- Social rights
- Economic rights
- Civic rights
- Cultural rights
- Language rights
- Religious rights
- Political rights
- Environmental rights

Key skills you will use in this chapter

- ✓ Being Creative
- ✓ Being Literate
- ✓ Being Numerate
- ✓ Communicating
- ✓ Managing Information and Thinking
- ✓ Managing Myself
- ✓ Staying Well
- ✓ Working with Others

Wellbeing indicators in this chapter

Classification of human rights

In the last chapter you examined some key human rights instruments or documents. You also examined some of the rights contained in these documents. These rights can be broadly divided into seven distinct classes or types.

❶ Social and economic rights

Social and economic rights ensure that every person can develop fully and lead a happy, healthy life. Such rights include the right to an adequate standard of living, the right to adequate housing, the right to food and clean water, the right to receive an education, the right to work and the right to healthcare. These rights are important because they ensure that our basic human needs are met. In Ireland, it is the government's responsibility to protect the social and economic rights of its citizens. The Department of Social Protection is one government department responsible for promoting the social welfare of its citizens.

Research

Go online and look at the Department of Social Protection website to see how this government department protects the social and economic rights of Irish citizens.

- ✓ Being Literate
- ✓ Communicating
- ✓ Managing Information and Thinking
- ✓ Managing Myself
- ✓ Staying Well
- ✓ Working with Others

❷ Civic rights

Civic rights refer to the freedoms we have as citizens or as members of communities. Civic rights enable individuals to participate effectively in society. It is important that we are aware of our civic rights, but also that we are aware of the responsibilities that come with them.

Civic rights include the right to liberty and freedom, the right to be treated equally and not discriminated against, the right to a nationality and freedom of travel.

Can you name some other civic rights?

❸ Cultural rights

Everyone has the right to enjoy and participate in cultural activities. Many people express culture through dress, traditions, song and art. **Cultural rights** recognise that human beings are entitled to express their culture without being discriminated against. In this way, the rights of cultural minorities are protected.

❹ Language rights

Thousands of languages are spoken all over the world. In Asia alone, more than 2,000 languages are spoken. **Language rights** mean that we all have the right to communicate in the language of our choice, either in private or in public, without discrimination.

Can you name five languages spoken in Europe?

❺ Religious rights

Religious rights enable individuals or groups to practise the religion of their choice. This involves the right to go to a place of worship and observe the rituals associated with that religion. Individuals also have the freedom to change religion or have no religious beliefs at all.

Can you name a country where there is religious conflict?

❻ Political rights

Political rights assure our right to participate in the political life of the country we live in. Political rights safeguard our right to vote, to hold public office and to take part in political activities. The government plays an important role in ensuring that citizens benefit from political rights.

Can you describe a situation, either past or present, when political rights were not respected by a government?

7 Environmental rights

We all depend on the environment for our livelihood, our health and for access to basic needs such as food, water and air. **Environmental rights** mean that every person has the right to live in a clean and healthy environment. These rights give us the freedom to enjoy unspoilt natural resources.

Can you describe a natural disaster or human actions that have had a bad effect on the environmental rights of people?

Read the newspaper article below and answer the questions that follow.

Muslim woman told to remove hijab by police on French beach before being racially abused

Mother and children reduced to tears after being surrounded by crowd shouting 'Go home' and 'We're Catholics'.

A mother was told to remove her hijab or face being fined by police while relaxing on a beach in France, before reportedly being racially abused by locals.

The thirty-four-year-old former flight attendant, named only as Siam, was approached by three officers while at La Bocca beach in Cannes with her young children and was ordered to take off her floral-patterned headscarf.

Siam said the police read her the details of the headscarf ban on beaches, stating beachgoers must wear 'correct clothing, respect secularism, hygiene rules and security' and arguing that her hijab was an 'ostentatious' sign of religion.

The mother agreed to pay the €11 fine but was then reportedly surrounded by a crowd shouting 'Go home' and 'We're Catholics', reducing her to tears, according to witnesses.

'I wasn't there to provoke anyone. I was stunned – racist terms were used freely,' Siam told French news magazine *L'Obs*.

'My children were crying, witnessing the humiliation of me and my family. Even I could not help crying. They humiliated us.'

Mathilde Cusin, a journalist for France 4, observed the incident and said the crowd were like a 'pack of hounds' attacking the woman. 'People asked her to leave or remove her veil, it was pretty violent,' she said.

'What shocked me is that it was mostly people in their thirties, not the elderly as one might imagine.'

Mayor of Cannes David Lisnard supported the actions of the police officers, arguing they were right to fine anyone wearing a religious garment and had 'no reason to doubt their judgement'.

In a statement, the mayor said he did not wish any Muslims to feel unwelcome on the beach and said people of all faiths should be allowed their rights.

Siam meanwhile confirmed she planned to contest the case and said she had contacted the Collectif Contre L'Islamophobie, an organisation which protects the rights of Muslim citizens.

'In a country meant to be famed for its human rights, I haven't seen any evidence of the principles of *liberté*, *égalité* or *fraternité*,' she added.

A ban applies in France to any 'clothing showing religious faith in an ostentatious way that is capable of creating risks to public order'.

Source: The Independent

? ••• Questions

- Being Literate
- Managing Information and Thinking
- Managing Myself

1   What right or rights have been denied to Siam?

2   In what country did this incident take place?

3   What religion does Siam practise?

4   Why was Siam fined by the police?

5   Do you think that the police were right to do this? Why or why not?

6   Why did Siam feel humiliated?

7   What is the French law with regard to religious attire? What is the reasoning behind it?

8   Do you think that laws are always right? Explain your answer.

Take action!

- Being Creative
- Being Literate
- Communicating
- Managing Information and Thinking
- Working with Others

Now that you have learned about the different classes of rights, create a human rights gallery on your classroom wall.

Draw a picture or poster showing one of the seven classes of rights. Your picture or poster should have a visual that represents that class of right and a brief explanation of why that right is important.

Don't forget to complete your reflections in your reflective journal.

Human rights conflicts and abuses

Learning outcomes

By the end of this chapter you should be able to outline different perspectives where there is a conflict of rights and an abuse of rights.

Key words

- Conflict of rights
- Clash of rights
- Compromise
- Violated
- Death penalty
- Human rights abuse
- Capital punishment
- Contentious
- Perspectives
- Torture

Key skills you will use in this chapter

- ✓ Being Creative
- ✓ Being Literate
- ✓ Being Numerate
- ✓ Communicating
- ✓ Managing Information and Thinking
- ✓ Managing Myself
- ✓ Staying Well
- ✓ Working with Others

Wellbeing indicators in this chapter

Clash of rights

In some situations, more than one person's rights need to be taken into consideration. When this happens, there can be a **conflict of rights** or a **clash of rights**. A clash of rights can cause conflict. To avoid further conflict or disagreements, both sides must take responsibility to come together to find a solution. This may involve a **compromise**. A compromise occurs when both sides respect each other's rights, and differences are settled. This may involve both sides making concessions (giving in to demands) so that an agreement can be reached. A compromise ensures that further conflict is avoided.

Read the following scenarios and suggest a suitable compromise for each one.

Scenario 1

Ryan is studying in his bedroom. His brother Michael is downstairs practising his electric guitar. He has his guitar hooked up to speakers and the noise is distracting Ryan from his studies. Ryan goes downstairs and asks Michael to stop. Michael refuses.

Can you suggest a suitable compromise?

Scenario 2

Karen is a factory owner. Her factory is located near a housing estate. The factory is important to the local community because it provides employment. Some of the residents have noticed a bad smell coming from the factory. Karen knows this but she doesn't have the money to solve the problem immediately. The residents have told their concerns to the residents' association. The residents' association is planning to hold a protest outside the factory.

Can you suggest a suitable compromise?

Scenario 3

Ann Marie and Conor live next door to each other. Ann Marie is a keen gardener and takes pride in her back garden with its many shrubs and trees. One of the trees has grown very high and has begun to block the light into Conor's kitchen. Conor is unhappy about this because he has to turn the lights on in his kitchen during the daytime. He has asked Ann Marie to do something about the situation but Ann Marie has refused.

Can you suggest a suitable compromise?

Role play

 Being Creative
 Communicating
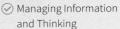 Managing Information and Thinking
Managing Myself
Working with Others

Oisín and Kasia live next door to each other. Oisín recently moved into his house and has had a few housewarming parties. The parties involved loud music and noisy party-goers. The parties often went on into the early hours. Kasia has two young children. They have woken up during the night because of the parties and were tired and cranky going to school in the morning. Kasia understands that Oisín is young and wants to have fun, but it is getting to be too much for her.

Choose two people to act out the roles of Kasia and Oisín. During the role play, both characters should tell their side of the story to the other. Each character should listen carefully to understand the other's point of view. During the role play it is important that both characters try to reach a compromise with each other.

Research

Being Creative
Being Literate
Managing Information and Thinking
Managing Myself

Northern Ireland has experienced conflict due a clash of political, religious and cultural rights.

Research the role of the Northern Ireland Parades Commission and its attempts to find a compromise to the parades conflict between the nationalist and loyalist communities. Write a report on your findings.

The Covid-19 pandemic

The Covid-19 pandemic is one of the greatest global challenges ever experienced. To stop the spread of the virus and to protect their most vulnerable citizens, governments around the world introduced restrictions that affected the everyday lives of people. Many countries were put under 'lockdown'. In Ireland, schools were closed, businesses were shut down, sports facilities were closed, and older people were advised to stay indoors. Travel restrictions were also introduced, and masks became mandatory for people shopping or availing of indoor services. People were encouraged to stay home and stay safe.

Level 5 Covid-19 Restrictions

No visits to homes or gardens

Those living alone can form a support bubble with one other household

You can meet one other household in an outdoor setting such as a park

Stay within 5 km of home (apart from listed reasons)

Work at home unless providing essential service requiring physical presence

Schools and childcare services will remain open

Professional, elite sports and intercounty Gaelic games, horse racing and greyhound racing can continue behind closed doors

Non-contact training can continue outdoors for school-age children in pods of 15

Up to 25 people can attend a wedding (indoors or outdoors)

Religious services should be online, but up to 25 people can attend funerals

Pubs, cafés, restaurants: takeaway or delivery only. Wet pubs in Dublin remain closed.

Only essential retail and services can remain open

COVID-19 restrictions in Ireland at Level 5

Some people felt that these restrictions were too harsh and that the restrictions denied citizens their human rights and freedoms. This presented a conflict between the right of the government to protect the health of the nation, and the rights of individuals. In Ireland and other countries, numerous protests took place to end the lockdown.

Protesters outside the GPO in Dublin, September 2020

 Questions

1   Study the infographic on Level 5 Covid-19 restrictions. List five restrictions outlined in the infographic.

2   Study the UDHR on page 69. Name three rights that were restricted or taken away because of lockdowns.

3   Do you think the Covid-19 restrictions were justified? Write a paragraph explaining your answer.

- ⊘ Being Creative
- ⊘ Being Literate
- ⊘ Managing Information and Thinking
- ⊘ Managing Myself

Human rights abuses: Focus on the death penalty

Despite the existence of human rights documents that seek to protect the rights of every human being, many people around the world experience human rights abuses. Human rights abuses occur when human rights are **violated** or taken away. Article 3 of the UN Declaration of Human Rights states that every person has the right to life and liberty, but there are many situations where this fundamental right is abused or violated. We will now explore the **death penalty**, which many believe is a key **human rights abuse**.

The death penalty is also known as **capital punishment**. Every year, thousands of men, women and sometimes even children are executed. Some have committed murder, others have committed minor crimes and some no crime at all. Today many people are on 'death row' in prisons waiting for their execution.

They don't know if they will see their families again or when they will be executed.

Capital punishment (legally allowing someone to be killed as a punishment for a crime) is not allowed in most countries, but it still exists in many. Study the map below, which highlights the countries that still have the death penalty.

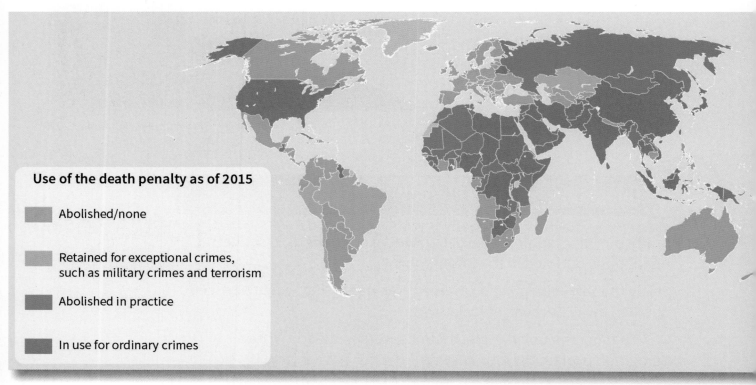

Use of the death penalty as of 2015

Abolished/none

Retained for exceptional crimes, such as military crimes and terrorism

Abolished in practice

In use for ordinary crimes

Use of the death penalty around the world (source: Amnesty International and press reports)

? Questions

⊘ Being Literate
⊘ Managing Information and Thinking
⊘ Managing Myself

Study the map above and answer the following questions in your copybook. Use your atlas to help you if necessary.

1   Name five counties that use capital punishment for ordinary crimes.

2   Name the only country in Europe that has the death penalty.

Methods of execution

The most common forms of execution are:

- 🌐 Beheading
- 🌐 Lethal injection
- 🌐 Hanging
- 🌐 Electrocution
- 🌐 Death by firing squad.

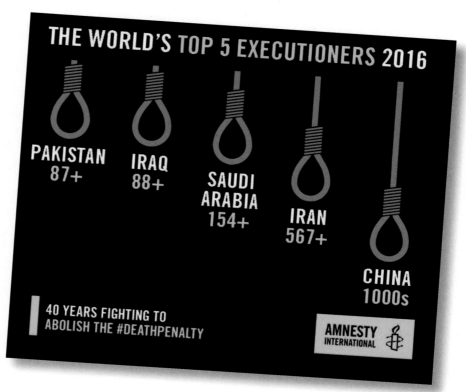

THE WORLD'S TOP 5 EXECUTIONERS 2016

PAKISTAN
87+

IRAQ
88+

SAUDI
ARABIA
154+

IRAN
567+

CHINA
1000s

40 YEARS FIGHTING TO
ABOLISH THE #DEATHPENALTY

AMNESTY
INTERNATIONAL

Different perspectives on the death penalty

The death penalty has always been a **contentious** issue. A contentious issue is an issue that people argue about. This is because there is a lot of disagreement as to whether or not the death penalty can be justified. We will now explore some different **perspectives** about the death penalty.

Those who are in favour of the death penalty argue that:

- 🌐 The death penalty is a deterrent (something that discourages) for serious crimes such as murder.
- 🌐 The death penalty ensures justice for victims of serious crimes such as murder.
- 🌐 The death penalty provides some form of closure for the families of murder victims.
- 🌐 The punishment should fit the crime. If an individual commits murder, this leads to the death of the victim. Therefore, death should be the punishment.
- 🌐 Once someone commits murder, they have given up their rights, including the right to life.

Those who are against the death penalty argue that:

- The death penalty denies an individual their right to life.

- Execution and the death penalty cannot be reversed. Sometimes people convicted of crimes are later found to be innocent.

- The justice system is corrupt in some countries. People have been put to death because of confessions that have been obtained through **torture**. In addition, men, women and children have been executed for minor crimes.

- Some countries use the death penalty as a way of getting rid of political opponents. Often these people have committed no serious crimes.

- There is no evidence that the death penalty reduces serious crime.

Can you think of some other arguments for or against the death penalty?

The work of Amnesty International

Amnesty International is a human rights organisation that has been campaigning against the death penalty since 1977. Amnesty International calls for the following:

- Countries that still have the death penalty should stop all executions.

- Countries that have recently abolished the death penalty need to remove it from their law books permanently.

- Death sentences should be commuted (changed) to prison sentences.

One of the ways Amnesty International campaigns against the death penalty is through letter-writing campaigns. Many letter-writing campaigns organised by Amnesty International have put pressure on governments around the world. Their campaigns have resulted in the abolition of the death penalty in many countries. These campaigns remind us of

the importance of standing up for the rights of others and how effective it can be. One letter really can make all the difference!

Debate

Organise a walking debate on the following topic:

 'The death penalty is justified in some cases.'

In the course of the debate, did your opinion change?
Can you explain why?

- ⊘ Being Creative
- ⊘ Being Literate
- ⊘ Communicating
- ⊘ Managing Information and Thinking
- ⊘ Managing Myself
- ⊘ Working with Others

Take action!

- ⊘ Being Creative
- ⊘ Being Literate
- ⊘ Communicating
- ⊘ Managing Information and Thinking

Look again at the map on page 86 that highlights countries that still use the death penalty.

Pick one of these countries. Find out the name of the leader of this country. Write a letter to this leader using the template in your reflective journal, outlining three reasons why, in your opinion, the death penalty is wrong.

Don't forget to complete your reflections in your reflective journal.

Taking responsibility for human rights

Learning outcomes

By the end of this chapter you should understand the importance of defending your own human rights and those of others.

Key words

- Responsibilities
- Responsible citizen
- Human rights
- Action
- Citizenship action

Key skills you will use in this chapter

- ✓ Being Creative
- ✓ Being Literate
- ✓ Being Numerate
- ✓ Communicating
- ✓ Managing Information and Thinking
- ✓ Managing Myself
- ✓ Staying Well
- ✓ Working with Others

Wellbeing indicators in this chapter

Taking responsibility

While it is important to be aware of our rights, it is equally important that we don't lose track of our **responsibilities** to ourselves and others. Not taking our responsibilities seriously means that we can act in selfish ways that ignore or disrespect the rights of others. As a result, the rights of others are denied or violated.

As individuals we need to think carefully about our words and actions and how they affect others.

The following poem by Pastor Martin Niemöller outlines the consequences of not taking responsibility for the rights of others. The poem describes the persecution of different groups by the Nazis during the Second World War.

Study the poem below. As a class, discuss the key message in this poem and how this poem applies to our lives today.

Pastor Martin Niemöller

First They Came
by Pastor Martin Niemöller

First they came for the Communists

And I did not speak out

Because I was not a Communist

Then they came for the Socialists

And I did not speak out

Because I was not a Socialist

Then they came for the trade unionists

And I did not speak out

Because I was not a trade unionist

Then they came for the Jews

And I did not speak out

Because I was not a Jew

Then they came for me

And there was no one left

To speak out for me.

Responsible citizenship

Taking responsibility for our own rights and the rights of others involves responsible citizenship. **Responsible citizens** participate in their communities and strive to make the world a better place.

What does responsible citizenship involve?

Respecting the rights of others

GIVE RESPECT
****
EARN RESPECT

Helping and caring for the most vulnerable in society

Treating others as we would like to be treated

Listening to and respecting other people's opinions or points of view

Respecting the natural environment

Taking care of community facilities and amenities

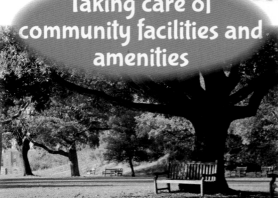

Highlighting injustices in the community and the wider world

How can I defend human rights?

Defending **human rights** is not just the responsibility of governments and human rights instruments. Defending human rights is everyone's business. We all have a responsibility to defend not only our own human rights, but those of others too.

Think, pair and share

In Chapter 2 you explored the issue of bullying. Bullying denies individuals the right to feel safe and secure. If you were a victim of bullying, what action could you take to protect this right?

Write your thoughts down. Now turn to your partner. Listen to their thoughts. Are there similarities or differences between your ideas? Decide what information you will share with the class group. Use the table in your reflective journal to write down your ideas.

- ⊘ Being Creative
- ⊘ Being Literate
- ⊘ Communicating
- ⊘ Managing Information and Thinking
- ⊘ Managing Myself
- ⊘ Staying Well
- ⊘ Working with Others

There are numerous ways in which you can play a role in defending human rights at home or abroad. Let's explore some of them.

① Join a human rights organisation

There are many human rights organisations in Ireland and abroad that try to protect and defend human rights. These organisations not only raise awareness about human rights, but also run campaigns to highlight human rights abuses throughout the world. By joining such organisations and getting involved with their campaigns, you will be playing an active role in defending human rights.

❷ Volunteer in your community

Volunteering means giving up your free time and energy to improve the lives of people in your community. Volunteering can involve defending the human rights of others. Numerous volunteers provide soup runs for the homeless, look after the elderly and provide services for people with disabilities, for example. In taking action to help others, volunteers make their communities a better place and make a positive difference in the lives of others.

▶ **Video** Volunteer Ireland – Who we are

❸ Fundraise for a charity or a human rights organisation

Many charities and human rights organisations rely on donations to carry out their work. Many of these organisations rely on the fundraising activities of their supporters in their efforts to protect or promote human rights. By organising a fundraising event, you are helping organisations to help others. There are many ways in which you can fundraise for an organisation. These include:

- 🌐 Cake sales
- 🌐 Sales of work
- 🌐 Sponsored walks or cycles
- 🌐 Raffles
- 🌐 Quizzes.

❹ Organise or participate in peaceful protests

Sometimes protests are organised to highlight an injustice or a human rights issue. By participating in a protest, you are using your voice to speak out against human rights injustices at home or in the wider world. Mass protests are effective in raising awareness about human rights abuses. This is because they often gain media attention, which raises awareness about the human rights issue.

5 Organise or sign a petition

A petition is a document, signed by people, that calls for change or action. When petitions get the required number of signatures, they are usually presented to a government or public representative. When you sign a petition, you are supporting a call for change. Many human rights organisations use petitions as a way to promote and defend human rights worldwide. In some

cases, petitions call for an end to human rights abuses or to change a law that denies individuals or groups their human rights. In this digital age, petitions have become more widespread. This is because many petitions can be signed online. You can set up your own petition on websites such as Change.org.

6 Raise awareness about a human rights issue

Sometimes people are not aware of human rights issues, so there is a need to raise awareness about them. There are many awareness-raising activities in which you can take part. These include:

- ⊕ Organising a poster campaign
- ⊕ Organising a school or public meeting

- ⊕ Inviting a guest speaker with knowledge of that issue to speak to students and/or parents in your school
- ⊕ Giving a presentation about a human rights issue.

7 Lobby public representatives

Lobbying involves putting pressure on public representatives such as TDs and councillors to do something about a situation that denies individuals or groups their rights. Lobbying can take many forms. It can involve letter-writing, emails, phone calls or meeting TDs and councillors in their local clinics. Any person, young or old, can lobby a politician on a particular issue.

Taking action

Taking **action** involves doing something to bring about a positive change in your community, the state or the wider world. By taking action, you can help to make a difference to people's lives and help to promote, protect or raise awareness about human rights. Taking action is not just for adults. Many young people in Ireland and throughout the world have taken action to make a difference. Your study of CSPE will give you an opportunity to reflect on issues that affect you and others and will help you to develop the skills required for active and responsible citizenship.

You are required to undertake at least three **citizenship actions** across the three strands of CPSE. These actions help to develop the skills necessary for active citizenship. On pages 97–98, read the two examples of actions that schools have undertaken as part of their CSPE course.

 ## Take action!

✓ Being Literate
✓ Communicating
✓ Managing Information and Thinking
✓ Managing Myself

Track the media for stories or news reports about individuals or groups who are taking responsibility for defending human rights.

 Don't forget to complete your reflections in your reflective journal.

Sample citizenship action 1: Organising a shoebox appeal for schools

We were learning about children's rights and how millions of children throughout the world are denied basic human rights. As a class, we felt we needed to something to help these children. One of my classmates told the class about an organisation called Team Hope that works with vulnerable children overseas. He told us that this organisation organises a shoebox appeal every Christmas that helps collect educational materials, personal hygiene products and clothing for children in the developing world. Everyone in our class agreed that we would like to organise a shoebox appeal in our school.

We organised ourselves into teams or committees to undertake this action. The permission committee ran this idea past the principal, who thought it was a great idea. The public relations committee designed posters and leaflets that highlighted the shoebox appeal and outlined some of the items that should be included in each shoebox. A collection team organised a collection point in our school where students, parents and teachers could drop off their shoeboxes. The contact committee arranged these shoeboxes to be collected by a representative from Team Hope.

The shoebox appeal was a great success. We collected over 120 shoeboxes full of supplies! We hope our shoeboxes have made a difference to 120 children in the developing world.

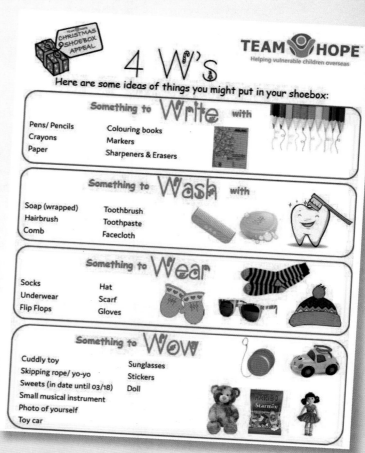

Sample citizenship action 2: A celebration of Human Rights Day

When our class was learning about human rights, we found out that Human Rights Day is celebrated every year on 10 December. Our class felt we needed to do something to celebrate or mark that important day. When we were brainstorming about possible actions we could undertake, one of our classmates pointed out that freedom of expression is one of our most important rights, so maybe we could do something to promote freedom of expression in our school. Everyone thought it was a good idea. We decided that we would create a 'freedom wall' in our school where students could freely write down what human rights meant to them. We asked the principal for permission and she was more than happy to let us go ahead with this action. She gave us a blank notice board in the school hall and advised us to cover it with paper.

Once we got permission, we set about planning and organising our action. To do this, we divided into committees. One committee was responsible for organising the freedom wall. They sourced paper from the art teacher and got markers so that students could write on the wall. Another committee had responsibility for public relations. They had to tell students in our school about the freedom wall. They designed posters and visited classes to highlight our action. Another committee had to organise a timetable for classes to visit and write on the freedom wall. On the day of the action, another committee manned the freedom wall and explained to students what they had to do.

Overall, the action was a success. It enabled students in our school to express what human rights meant to them and also highlighted the importance of the right to freedom of expression.

Strand 1: Suggested actions

Now take action to enhance your learning.

The following are suggested actions that are linked mainly to Strand 1.

 Use digital technology to create a display showing situations or cases where human dignity was or is being respected. Display your finished work in school or online.

 Article 12 of the United Nations Convention on the Rights of the Child states that 'Young people have the right to have their voices heard and for adults to listen and take them seriously in matters that affect them'. Examine how your school supports listening to and involving young people in decision-making about matters that affect them in school. Share your findings.

 Identify a human rights issue of concern and engage with an individual, group, organisation or campaign focusing on that issue.

 Lobby a relevant government department about a human rights issue of personal relevance and/or concern to young people.

 Design and conduct a survey to find out what peers/family members know and think about an issue relevant to human rights or children's rights. Share your findings with survey participants and with someone of influence.

Publish an article, blog, vlog or podcast (or similar) about the treatment of a minority group in Ireland, referencing one or more human rights instruments and/or equality legislation that is relevant to the issue.

 Organise a celebration to mark International Human Rights Day to inform people about the UDHR, UNCRC or ECHR, and/or organisations working in the field of human rights in Ireland. Research the impact of one global challenge (such as Covid-19, biodiversity loss, climate change, poverty) on the human rights of children and young people in Ireland or in the Global South.

 Organise a guest speaker(s) to talk to your class/school about a human rights or children's rights issue of interest/concern.

STRAND 2
GLOBAL CITIZENSHIP

In this strand you will explore issues of poverty, inequality and sustainable development. You will also look at ways to bring about effective change.

Unit 3   SUSTAINABILITY

Sustainability means meeting our present-day needs without endangering the ability of future generations to meet their own needs.

Chapter 11: How we connect with ecosystems
Chapter 12: Sustainable development
Chapter 13: My ecological footprint
Chapter 14: Sustainable strategies to help our planet

Unit 4   LOCAL AND GLOBAL DEVELOPMENT

Development can be a positive and negative influence on people's lives. It can be looked at on a local level and on a global level. Development is influenced by both individuals and institutions.

Chapter 15: The reality of poverty and inequality
Chapter 16: The causes of poverty
Chapter 17: Local development

Unit 5   EFFECTING GLOBAL CHANGE

Our planet is in a constant state of change. We have a role to play in this change. Change can have many causes and consequences. Active citizens campaign for change that is sustainable and positive.

Chapter 18: Power and influence
Chapter 19: An analysis of a global issue: Climate change
Chapter 20: Responsible consumption and production
Chapter 21: A campaign for change

How we connect with ecosystems

Learning outcomes

By the end of this chapter you will understand your connections to ecosystems, people and places both near and far. You will also understand how you depend on these connections.

Key skills you will use in this chapter

- ✓ Being Creative
- ✓ Being Literate
- ✓ Being Numerate
- ✓ Communicating
- ✓ Managing Information and Thinking
- ✓ Managing Myself
- ✓ Staying Well
- ✓ Working with Others

Key words

- Sustainable
- Active citizens
- Ecosystem
- Climate change
- Butterfly effect
- Unsustainable
- Fossil fuels
- Extreme weather
- Greenhouse gases
- Carbon dioxide (CO_2)
- Emissions
- Biodiversity
- Connected

- Interdependence
- Slave labour
- Inequality
- Exploited
- Child labour
- Domestic service
- Debt bondage
- Illicit activities
- Morally reprehensible
- Violate
- Informal sector
- Fair trade
- Commodities

Wellbeing indicators in this chapter

Sustainability

If something is **sustainable**, it should last for a very long time. In order to sustain something, we need to keep and support it for the future.

Active citizens try to live their lives in a sustainable way. This means we live in a way that enables all of us to survive and thrive. Try to take no more than you need. Try not to harm life or the environment. However, if you do cause some harm, make an effort to undo that harm or do something positive to help the world.

Think, pair and share

Think about your understanding of sustainability. What is your understanding of the word?

Write down your definition of sustainability in your reflective journal. Now turn to your partner. Listen to their definition. Are there similarities or differences? With your partner, decide on a definition you both agree on. Share that definition with your class group. Use the table in your reflective journal to write down your ideas.

- ✓ Being Creative
- ✓ Being Literate
- ✓ Communicating
- ✓ Managing Information and Thinking
- ✓ Managing Myself
- ✓ Staying Well
- ✓ Working with Others

Ecosystems

An **ecosystem** is all the living things, including plants, animals and small micro-organisms, that share an environment. An ecosystem can be as small as a single tree or as large as an entire forest.

The word *eco* describes anything to do with the environment and your connection to it. Humans depend on ecosystems and can be part of ecosystems. We have an important role to play in ecosystems.

Ecosystems provide humans with much support. For example, soil and crops are necessities for humans and each of these shares its ecosystem with us. Bees help pollinate plants and without them many species would not exist.

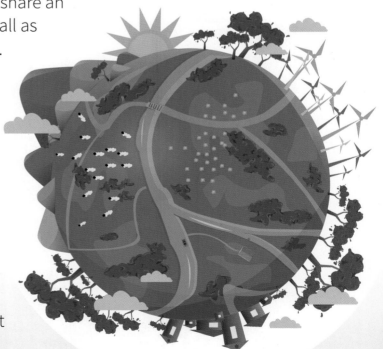

? ... Questions

⊘ Being Literate
⊘ Managing Information and Thinking
⊘ Managing Myself

1 Think about how humans positively influence our ecosystems. In your copybook, write down three steps humans can take and explain why they are positive.

2 Think about how humans can have a negative impact on ecosystems. Now write down three examples and explain why you think they are negative.

How we are connected to and depend on ecosystems

Impact of climate change

Climate change has been causing severe weather events in Ireland in recent years. We have experienced long cold spells, droughts and flooding. The impact of these extreme weather events depends on the ecosystems and on the condition of those ecosystems.

For example, flooding is a natural event, but when it affects the areas we live in, it can cause severe hardship.

Events such as flooding are not just a result of local conditions. They can be triggered by some event in another part of the world. This is sometimes referred to as the **'butterfly effect'**.

Often people living in an **unsustainable** way in one part of the world can contribute to problems such as flooding in another part of the world.

▶ **Video** The butterfly effect

Climate experts believe that burning **fossil fuels** (e.g. coal, oil) contributes to overheating the Earth, which can cause an increase in **extreme weather** such as storms and coastal flooding. Burning these fossil fuels produces large amounts of pollution known as **greenhouse gases**. These gases have had a serious effect on raising temperatures around the world, particularly over the past fifty years.

The main greenhouse gas is **carbon dioxide (CO_2)**. When fossil fuels are burned:

🌐 They release huge amounts of CO_2 into the atmosphere.

🌐 These high levels of CO_2 absorb heat from the Earth's surface, so less heat escapes from the atmosphere.

🌐 This means that the temperature rises and the Earth becomes warmer.

🌐 This increases evaporation of water, which leads to more rain.

🌐 This increased heating of the Earth also means more frequent and intense storms.

The main contributors to climate change are countries that have lots of industry. The countries producing the highest **emissions** of dangerous greenhouse gases in recent times are China, the United States and India.

Greenhouse effect

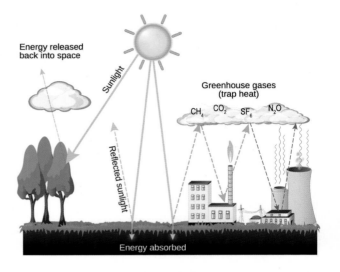

Energy released back into space

Sunlight

Reflected sunlight

Greenhouse gases (trap heat)

CH_4 CO_2 SF_6 N_2O

Energy absorbed

Group activity

- Being Creative
- Being Literate
- Communicating
- Managing Information and Thinking
- Managing Myself
- Working with Others

In groups of four, do the following:

✦ Share your ideas as to why flooding has become more frequent in Ireland in recent years. Consider how what happens in one part of the world can influence what happens elsewhere.

✦ Discuss in your group how humans all over the world can interact with their ecosystems in order to reduce the problem of flooding.

The rainforest ecosystem

The world's rainforests are spectacular because they contain a wide range of plants, species, people and resources. Rainforests have great biodiversity. **Biodiversity** means a large variety of plant and animal life can be found. The more biodiverse a place is, the richer its resources are.

Scientists have managed to study less than 1% of rainforest species, but from these studies they have been able to improve the lives of people across the world. For example, 25% of the world's medicines have been developed from resources found in rainforests. Scientists estimate that 70% of plants they have studied have anti-cancer properties. Undiscovered properties in the world's rainforests could help create cures for some of our most common diseases.

This is the Madagascar periwinkle plant. Scientists have used its properties to create two important cancer-fighting drugs. They are used to treat childhood leukaemia and Hodgkin's disease.

Madagascar periwinkle

Rainforests are also important to people all over the world because they can clean the air of dangerous greenhouse gases such as CO_2. Rainforests are sometimes called the 'lungs of our planet' because the large number of hardwood trees can take in vast quantities of CO_2. They act as a filter to clean the gas from our atmosphere. For example, it is estimated that more than 20% of the Earth's oxygen is created in the Amazon rainforest of South America.

Unfortunately, since 1950, over half of the world's rainforests have been destroyed by humans. Environmental studies show that more than 200,000 acres of rainforest are destroyed every day.

? Questions

1 Can you suggest one other negative impact humans have on the world's rainforests?

2 How, do you think, do the world's rainforests impact on our wellbeing?

3 Study the graph on deforestation in your reflective journal and answer the questions on it there.

- ⊘ Being Literate
- ⊘ Being Numerate
- ⊘ Managing Information and Thinking
- ⊘ Managing Myself
- ⊘ Staying Well

Research

- ✓ Being Creative
- ✓ Being Literate
- ✓ Communicating
- ✓ Managing Information and Thinking
- ✓ Managing Myself
- ✓ Working with Others

Go online to research the many ways in which humans are destroying the world's rainforests.

You could also find out about some organisations that actively encourage people to protect the rainforests. Be sure to record your findings according to your teacher's instructions and report back to your class.

We are connected to people both near and far

Interdependence

How we are connected to and depend on people and places

There is a saying, 'no man is an island'. This means that no one person exists in isolation. We are all **connected** to people and depend on people both near and far. Likewise, other people, both near to us and far away from us, depend on us. A word often used to describe this relationship between people is **interdependence**.

It is easy for us to name people we are connected to in our locality. For example, we are all members of local communities and we connect with people from our local communities every day. At the moment, you are connecting with your classmates and teachers. During class, you will also depend on these people, as they will depend on you.

We are all interconnected

Imagine!

You are connected to and depend on many people in your community.

Examples of other people in your locality who you depend on and are connected to:

- ⊘ Being Creative
- ⊘ Being Literate
- ⊘ Communicating
- ⊘ Managing Information and Thinking
- ⊘ Managing Myself
- ⊘ Working with Others

A farmer *A supermarket worker*

A postal worker

In your copybook, name five other people you are connected to and depend on in your local community.

Think, pair and share

Think about the ways you might be connected to each of the people in the photographs above.

Now turn to your partner. Listen to their ideas. As a pair, discuss how each of these people can go about their work in a sustainable way. Share your ideas with the rest of the class group. Use the table in your reflective journal to write down your ideas.

- ⊘ Being Creative
- ⊘ Being Literate
- ⊘ Communicating
- ⊘ Managing Information and Thinking
- ⊘ Managing Myself
- ⊘ Staying Well
- ⊘ Working with Others

Sometimes it is difficult for us to imagine that we are connected to and depend on people we have never met and who may live far away from us. For example, when you meet with your friends in a local coffee shop, do you ever wonder who has had an input into producing the hot chocolate or cappuccino you drink? What about your school uniform? Where was it made? Could it have been someone your own age, working in terrible conditions?

Joshua, a child labourer

Joshua is twelve years of age and lives near the city of Abengourou in the eastern part of the Ivory Coast, which is on the west coast of Africa.

Joshua has not been to school in the past four years and works extremely hard every day of the week at a stone mine. He has friends who have been taken from their families in Mali and Burkina Faso and forced to work on other plantations hundreds of kilometres away. This is known as **slave labour** and is a growing problem in West Africa.

Joshua would love to be in school because education would provide an escape for him. He would love to become an engineer and help to build better roads and schools in his home town.

The Ivory Coast, Mali and Burkina Faso

? Questions

1 How are you connected to Joshua?

2 How do you feel about this connection?

3 Do you think that this is a sustainable way of life for this young boy? Explain your answer.

4 How could you help to make a difference in the lives of children like Joshua?

⊘ Being Literate
⊘ Managing Information and Thinking
⊘ Managing Myself

Take action!

⊘ Being Literate
⊘ Communicating
⊘ Managing Myself
⊘ Working with Others

With your class, produce an information pack for your school community showing the plight of children like Joshua. You could do this in a digital format and ask permission from the school management to display it on your school website.

When we consider our connections to people living in other parts of the world, we often begin to realise that there is a lot of **inequality** in the world. Sometimes, in order for us to have the things we want, other people have to do things that make their lives quite difficult. When young children are forced to work in difficult conditions and are **exploited**, we refer to this as **child labour**.

The following is a United Nations definition of child labour:

> 'It is work that children should not be doing because they are too young to work, or – if they are old enough to work – because it is dangerous or otherwise unsuitable for them.'

It goes on to say:

> 'There are many forms of child labour worldwide. Children are engaged in agricultural labour, in mining, in manufacturing, in domestic service, types of construction, scavenging and begging on the streets. Others are trapped in forms of slavery in armed conflicts, forced labour and debt bondage (to pay off debts incurred by parents and grandparents) as well as in commercial sexual exploitation and illicit activities, such as drug trafficking and organised begging and in many other forms of labour. Many of these are "worst forms" of child labour as they are especially harmful, morally reprehensible, and they violate the child's freedom and human rights. Child labour tends to be concentrated in the informal sector of the economy. For some work, children receive no payment, only food and a place to sleep. Children in informal sector work receive no payment if they are injured or become ill, and can seek no protection if they suffer violence or are maltreated by their employer.'

Child labour

Child soldier

Debate

Organise a walking debate on one of the following topics:

💬 'Our actions can contribute to the problem of child labour.'

💬 'We should not buy products from shops or cafés that source their material from countries where child labour takes place.'

💬 'Our choices can make the world a more sustainable place.'

Having completed the debate, has your opinion remained the same or has it changed? Can you explain why?

Copy the following KWL table in your copybook to help you record the process.

✓ Being Creative
✓ Being Literate
✓ Communicating
✓ Managing Information and Thinking
✓ Managing Myself
✓ Working with Others

K What I knew before the debate	**W** What I wanted to know more about	**L** What I learned more about

The fair trade movement

We can make a difference to the lives of people who are being exploited if we consider our actions. One simple way to make such a difference is to insist on buying goods we know have not been created by exploiting others in places far away. Many movements are now actively helping to stop the exploitation of these people. One such movement is the **fair trade** movement.

The Fairtrade Mark

The fair trade movement started when consumers began to realise that the people who produce our food are often not paid fairly for their hard work and are exploited by trading relationships. Fair trade tries to address this by ensuring that producers, especially those in the least economically developed countries, receive a fair price for producing **commodities** such as rice, sugar, coffee, tea and bananas.

When you see the Fairtrade Mark, it means that producers are getting a better deal from what they sell. When you buy items with the Fairtrade logo, you know that you are making a positive difference to the lives of these people.

Cocoa farmers and workers

Chocolate is one of the world's favourite foods but growing cocoa is a hard task. The fair trade movement is helping to make it more sustainable.

Take action!

- ✓ Being Literate
- ✓ Communicating
- ✓ Managing Information and Thinking
- ✓ Managing Myself
- ✓ Working with Others

The fair trade movement connects people who depend on us and on whom we depend.

Contact Fairtrade Ireland and invite them to send a guest speaker to your school. The guest speaker will be able to help you and your classmates to understand how the fair trade movement is helping to develop a more sustainable way of life for people in less developed regions of the world.

 Don't forget to complete your reflections in your reflective journal.

Sustainable development

Learning outcomes

By the end of this chapter you will understand what is meant by the term *development*. You will also be able to explain the idea of sustainable development and how it can be positive for people.

Key skills you will use in this chapter

- ✓ **Being Creative**
- ✓ **Being Literate**
- ✓ **Being Numerate**
- ✓ **Communicating**
- ✓ **Managing Information and Thinking**
- ✓ **Managing Myself**
- ✓ **Staying Well**
- ✓ **Working with Others**

Key words

- Development
- Social development
- Economic development
- Quality of life
- Celtic Tiger
- Sustainable development
- Planning permission

Wellbeing indicators in this chapter

Throughout the world, people's lives are constantly changing and developing. The speed of this change and **development** differs from community to community and from state to state. Change and development generally improve people's lives, but not always. Development is usually planned and often happens only when it helps the majority of people in an area. It can involve long-term, medium-term or short-term planning. However, it is also important to realise that development can cause conflict and create problems for communities and states.

Definition of development

Development can have different meanings in different situations.

🌐 **Social development** is when we make human needs a priority. We try to improve people's lives so that society can be better for everybody.

🌐 **Economic development** is when we make financial needs a priority. By improving the finances of a society, we can improve the lives of people.

Think, pair and share

- ✓ Being Creative
- ✓ Being Literate
- ✓ Communicating
- ✓ Managing Information and Thinking
- ✓ Managing Myself
- ✓ Working with Others

Think about development. What is your understanding of this word?

Write down your own definition of development in your reflective journal. Turn to your partner. Listen to their definition. Decide on a definition that you are both happy with. Report that definition to the class group. Use the table in your reflective journal to write down your ideas.

Social development

A good way to understand social development is to look at the **quality of life** people have in different situations. Quality of life can refer to how positive people's lives can be, for example if people have good health, access to education, access to housing, freedom to practise their religion and have access to employment.

Unfortunately, there are many instances where quality of life for people is very poor. Many people suffer from poor quality of life in our country and abroad. When society lacks social development, it has a negative effect on everybody.

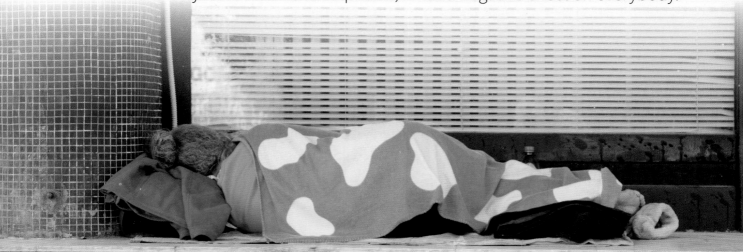

Debate

Organise a walking debate on the following topic:

  'Quality of life in Ireland is good and everybody benefits from it.'

Having completed the debate, has your opinion remained the same or has it changed? Can you explain why?

- ✓ Being Creative
- ✓ Being Literate
- ✓ Communicating
- ✓ Managing Information and Thinking
- ✓ Managing Myself
- ✓ Working with Others

Economic development

Economic development can mean many things to many people, but it mainly refers to how well a society is doing from a financial point of view. Economic development can be a very good thing for a society if it is managed properly. It can make people's lives better and help the government to invest in its services and its people.

Ireland experienced rapid economic development during the **Celtic Tiger** period. This was from the late 1990s to 2007. A result of this economic development was a massive boom in building throughout the country.

However, this economic development was not sustainable. Experts believe that we built too many houses and other properties too quickly. Economic growth takes time. When it happens too quickly, there can be problems.

When managed well, however, economic development can have very positive effects on a society. In Norway, large reserves of oil were discovered in the North Sea in the 1970s. Oil is a very important source of energy and the Norwegian government and its people used the oil to develop the economy. Norway is now one of the richest and most developed economies in the world. The Norwegians have invested the money in improving services and infrastructure and improving people's lives.

Imagine!

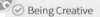

- Being Creative
- Being Literate
- Managing Information and Thinking
- Managing Myself

Imagine that a large amount of oil is discovered off the Irish coast.

1   In your copybook, list and briefly explain two positive outcomes of the discovery.

2   In your copybook, list and briefly explain two negative outcomes of the discovery.

Sustainable development

As we have seen, development can happen in many ways and can have positive and negative results. We need to make sure that development doesn't cause long-term damage to our environment.

We all have a responsibility to make sure that development is sustainable. It is only when we have a sustainable approach to development that we can be sure we are not damaging our environment and society.

Take a look at the following proposed development for a region in the midlands of Ireland.

An international holiday resort company wants to develop a holiday theme park in a beautiful woodland and lake region. It will cover more than 4,000 acres of woodlands and lakes. There will be more than 500 accommodation lodges. There will be bars and restaurants, an activity zone and, of course, rollercoasters and theme rides.

1   The **company** is not Irish-owned. It is a foreign multinational company and has similar parks throughout Europe. They have applied for **planning permission** from the local council.

2   The **owners** of the land will receive a large sum of money if the development gets planning permission. Some of the owners are interested in the money and some are concerned about the wildlife and its habitats.

3   There is a river near the proposed development, which is used by local **fishing enthusiasts, families and tourists**.

4   One local **TD** has agreed to help the company to explain the proposal to the local community.

5 A **local county councillor** is against the development.

6 Some **local farmers** are not happy with the proposed development.

7 The **local business group** has enthusiastically welcomed the proposed development.

8 The **planning committee** of the local county council will decide whether or not the development should go ahead.

Group activity

- Being Creative
- Being Literate
- Being Numerate
- Communicating
- Managing Information and Thinking
- Managing Myself
- Working with Others

Divide the class into eight groups corresponding with the groups mentioned above. Each group (except for the planning committee group) will put forward an argument in favour of or against the proposed development.

- A representative from each group will then present the argument to the class.
- The eighth group – the planning committee representing the local county council – will listen to all the arguments put forward.
- When all the arguments have been heard, the planning committee will give reasons why the development should or should not go ahead. Use the blank graph in your reflective journal to record the results.

- Being Creative
- Being Literate
- Managing Information and Thinking
- Managing Myself
- Staying Well
- Working with Others

Take action!

Design an awareness-raising campaign for your school on how to promote sustainable development in Ireland in the twenty-first century.

Don't forget to complete your reflections in your reflective journal.

My ecological footprint

Learning outcomes

By the end of this chapter you will understand what is meant by the term *ecological footprint*. You will be able to create a visual representation of your own ecological footprint.

Key skills you will use in this chapter

- ✓ Being Creative
- ✓ Being Literate
- ✓ Being Numerate
- ✓ Communicating
- ✓ Managing Information and Thinking
- ✓ Managing Myself
- ✓ Staying Well
- ✓ Working with Others

Key words

- Ecological footprint
- Hectares
- Carbon
- Cropland
- Grazing land
- Forest
- Built-up land
- Fishing grounds

Wellbeing indicators in this chapter

What is my ecological footprint?

Your **ecological footprint** refers to the impact that your activities have on the environment. In other words, how much of the environment do you use to sustain your lifestyle? It can be measured by how much nature it takes to support you. It is measured in global hectares. This means that we can estimate using **hectares** (a hectare is 10,000 square metres) how much of an impact our footprints have. We can then easily compare the impact different people and different countries have on the environment.

Carbon

Cropland

Fishing grounds

Grazing land

Built-up land

Forest

Our ecological footprints are measured in relation to:

🌐 **Carbon:** How much carbon we produce and use by burning fossil fuels

🌐 **Cropland:** The amount of land used to grow crops to feed people and animals

🌐 **Grazing land:** The amount of grassland used to feed animals that we use to provide us with meat and dairy products

🌐 **Forest:** The amount of woodlands needed to provide us with timber products

🌐 **Built-up land:** The amount of land covered by buildings, transportation and industry

🌐 **Fishing grounds:** The large areas of our oceans and rivers used to catch fish species.

Individual activity

Think carefully about the ways you create an ecological footprint. Consider the following.

- **Your food:** What type of food do you eat? Some food requires large amounts of resources to be produced. For example, between 500 and 4,000 litres of water are required to produce 1 kg of wheat. Every day we all consume wheat products, such as bread and pasta, without ever considering the ecological impact it has.

- **Your home:** The type of house you live in and the materials used to build the house add to your ecological footprint.

- **Your energy usage:** The size of your home and the type of heating system in it has an impact on your ecological footprint.

- **Your waste materials:** Do you generate a lot of waste that goes to landfill?

- **Your travel:** How far do you travel by car or bus every day? Do you share lifts?

To calculate your own ecological footprint, log on to the Ecological Footprint Calculator website from the Global Footprint Network. Take the ecological footprint survey, then record your ecological footprint in your reflective journal.

- ⊘ Being Creative
- ⊘ Being Literate
- ⊘ Being Numerate
- ⊘ Managing Information and Thinking
- ⊘ Managing Myself

Take action!

You and your classmates could run an awareness-raising campaign in your school. Your campaign could highlight the impact of students' ecological footprints.

You could also suggest ways in which students in your school could reduce their ecological footprints. A report of your awareness-raising campaign could be submitted to your school newsletter.

- ⊘ Being Literate
- ⊘ Communicating
- ⊘ Managing Myself
- ⊘ Working with Others

Don't forget to complete your reflections in your reflective journal.

Sustainable strategies to help our planet

Learning outcomes

By the end of this chapter you should understand and be able to discuss strategies that individuals, communities, business, agriculture and governments can use to address climate change.

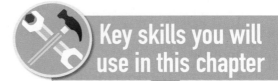

Key skills you will use in this chapter

- ✓ Being Creative
- ✓ Being Literate
- ✓ Being Numerate
- ✓ Communicating
- ✓ Managing Information and Thinking
- ✓ Managing Myself
- ✓ Staying Well
- ✓ Working with Others

Key words

- Sustainable strategies
- Reduce
- Replace
- Toxins
- Reuse
- Recycle
- Big business
- Carbon neutral
- Carbon negative
- Climate pledge
- Climate Action Plan
- Roadmap
- Climate neutral

Wellbeing indicators in this chapter

What can I do to address climate change?

We need to take a more sustainable approach to how we live our lives. Many of the things we do and the products we use can have a negative effect on our planet.

If we look at some of the following products people use on a daily basis, we can see how long it takes for these to be broken down so that they are no longer harmful to our environment.

**Tin can
+ 50 years**

**Styrofoam packaging
+ 50 years**

**Plastic take-away container
+ 50–80 years**

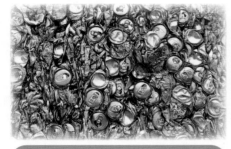

**Aluminium can
+ 200–500 years**

**Plastic bottle
+ 450 years**

**Disposable nappy
+ 550 years**

**Plastic bag
+ 200–1,000 years**

Video Plastic is not fantastic

Here are some **sustainable strategies** we can use to reduce our negative impact on the environment.

Strategy ❶ Reduce

Reducing the amount of waste you produce is the best way to help the environment. You and your family can do this in many different ways, such as buying products with little or no packaging. Some goods we buy are wrapped in layers of plastic and cardboard, while similar products can be bought with little or no packaging. If we opt to buy goods with less packaging, it means less energy is required to produce the product and less waste is produced.

Strategy ❷ Replace

Some products that we use every day are quite damaging to our environment. If we can **replace** these with similar products that are equally effective but less damaging to the environment, we will be taking a more sustainable approach to our environment.

For example, traditional household cleaners have **toxins** that are damaging and can be easily replaced with products that are environmentally friendly.

Strategy ❸ Reuse

We often buy new products when it is really not necessary to do so. For example, many of us use refuse sacks and shopping bags just once and then dispose of them. We could **reuse** these instead. Also, containers like empty take-away food containers and old shoe boxes can be cleaned and reused many times. By reusing products, we are taking a more sustainable approach.

Strategy ❹ Recycle

Many items we use every day can be **recycled**. This means the items can be used again in a different way. By recycling, we don't need to take more valuable resources from our planet. Items like aluminium cans and plastic bottles can be recycled – in some cases, many times over.

Video ReCreate – Creativity through reuse

Questions

1. Describe how you could use the four strategies to make a positive difference to the environment.

2. Describe two positive impacts a clean and healthy environment can have on wellbeing.

3. Describe two negative impacts an unhealthy and polluted environment can have on wellbeing.

- ⊘ Being Literate
- ⊘ Managing Information and Thinking
- ⊘ Managing Myself
- ⊘ Staying Well

Create a video

Divide the class into groups. Each group will create a short video clip on one of the sustainable strategies that can be used to help to improve your local environment.

- ⊘ Being Creative
- ⊘ Being Literate
- ⊘ Communicating
- ⊘ Managing Information and Thinking
- ⊘ Managing Myself
- ⊘ Working with Others

Take action!

Organise a campaign in your school to encourage students to reduce, replace, reuse and recycle.

- ⊘ Being Creative
- ⊘ Being Literate
- ⊘ Managing Information and Thinking
- ⊘ Managing Myself
- ⊘ Staying Well
- ⊘ Working with Others

How communities can address climate change

In Strand 1, you learned about communities to which you belong. Your school community is one of those communities. School communities can work successfully to address climate change. Small changes made by school communities over time can have a great effect. Many schools have Green-Schools committees. The aim of these is to promote action that is long-term and led by students, towards the goal of a sustainable environment. The students involve the local school community, and also try to involve other groups from their immediate community.

Green-Schools

Green-Schools is Ireland's leading environmental management and education programme for schools.

The Green-Schools programme focuses on various themes of sustainability. The themes are:

- ⊕ Litter & Waste
- ⊕ Energy
- ⊕ Water
- ⊕ Travel
- ⊕ Biodiversity
- ⊕ Global Citizenship

 Go to **www.greenschoolsireland.org** and research the projects that school communities can undertake to help tackle climate change. Report back to your class on your findings.

Each theme gets the students to take action to help improve the sustainability of the school. It is a terrific example of active citizenship. It encourages pride and responsibility among students as they help tackle climate change at a local level.

How business can address climate change

Business has a key role to play in addressing climate change. The planet needs **big business** to lead the way. Some of the world's largest companies produce more harmful emissions than some countries! For too many years, business has not shown leadership in tackling the climate crisis. However, if big business can lead the way, then there is great hope that we can make a more sustainable future for all.

Thankfully, some of the world's biggest companies have recently committed to strategies that will help.

- ⊕ **Carbon neutral** means that the amount of carbon an activity uses will be the same as the amount of carbon an activity releases. We can then say the activity has 'net zero' carbon emissions.

- ⊕ **Carbon negative** means an activity goes beyond achieving 'net zero' carbon emissions to actually create a benefit to the environment by removing additional carbon dioxide from the atmosphere.

- ⊕ **Big business** means a large profit-making company that is active all over the world.

Apple

Apple has committed to producing its technology without mining rare materials from the earth. The iPhone 12 used 100% recycled rare earth elements in all magnets contained in the phone, including the camera.

Amazon

In 2019, Amazon signed a **'climate pledge'** to be 100% carbon neutral by 2040. This means that the amount of carbon the company uses will be the same as the amount of carbon the company reduces. Amazon plans to invest in 100,000 electric trucks to help achieve this goal.

 Video Search online for a TED Talk video called 'Amazon's climate pledge to be net-zero by 2040' by Dave Clark and Kara Hurst.

Microsoft

Microsoft has committed to being 'carbon negative' by 2030. This means that Microsoft aims to remove more carbon from the atmosphere than it is emitting into the atmosphere.

Starbucks

Starbucks has committed to reducing its carbon emissions by 2030 and aims to store more carbon than it produces, making it a carbon negative business. One of the company's main strategies is to incorporate more plant-based dairy alternatives and plant-based ingredients.

Connect and communicate

- ⊘ Being Creative
- ⊘ Communicating
- ⊘ Managing Information and Thinking
- ⊘ Managing Myself
- ⊘ Working with Others

Connect and communicate with a company to investigate how it is tackling climate change.

Communicate by email, social media, letter or phone. Find out about the strategies the company has in place to address climate change. Ask if the company could arrange for one of its people to address your class via your school's learning platform (e.g. Google Classroom, Teams or Zoom).

How agriculture can address climate change

In 2019, 35% of Ireland's greenhouse gas emissions came from the agriculture sector, and 83% of emissions in the agriculture sector came from animals.

A plan was set out by the Department of Agriculture, Food and the Marine in 2021. It aims to make agriculture more sustainable in Ireland by using the following strategies to reduce emissions:

🌐 Setting targets to reduce fertiliser use

🌐 Encouraging lower-emitting cattle breeds

🌐 Promoting an increase in organic farming.

How government can address climate change

The government of Ireland published a **Climate Action Plan** in 2021. It contains a roadmap – a timeline showing goals and how these goals will be achieved. The plan aims to have a **climate neutral** economy by 2050. Climate neutral is similar to 'carbon neutral', but it also focuses on greenhouse gases other than carbon. (Methane is an example of one of these gases.) The state of being climate neutral can be achieved by dramatically reducing the amount of greenhouse gases released into the atmosphere. We will then balance the amount of gases still produced, by removing them through technology, our land and our forests.

Boglands and forests can store large amounts of carbon and can help reduce our carbon emissions

 **Take action!**

Create an infographic, video or report showing how big business/government/agriculture is being responsible and putting strategies in place to help address climate change.

⊘ Being Creative
⊘ Managing Information and Thinking
⊘ Being Literate
⊘ Being Numerate
⊘ Communicating
⊘ Working with Others

 Don't forget to complete your reflections in your reflective journal.

The reality of poverty and inequality

Learning outcomes

By the end of this chapter you will understand how people can experience poverty and inequality. You will understand that there are a variety of reasons why poverty and inequality exist. You will also be able to explain how certain people and organisations work towards overcoming poverty and inequality.

Key skills you will use in this chapter

- ✓ Being Creative
- ✓ Being Literate
- ✓ Being Numerate
- ✓ Communicating
- ✓ Managing Information and Thinking
- ✓ Managing Myself
- ✓ Staying Well
- ✓ Working with Others

Key words

- ⚷ Poverty
- ⚷ Inequality
- ⚷ Homeless
- ⚷ Rent allowance
- ⚷ Social welfare
- ⚷ Financial crisis
- ⚷ Humanitarian crisis
- ⚷ Impoverished

Wellbeing indicators in this chapter

As long as poverty, injustice and gross inequality persist in our world, none of us can truly rest.
-- Nelson Mandela

Poverty and inequality are familiar problems in society, despite all the wealth and resources available. These issues occur throughout the world in regions that are considered poor, but also in regions that are considered wealthy. Indeed, many people in our own country suffer poverty and inequality. We will now look at two case studies that highlight both.

Video No one should be left behind

Case study 1

In this example, we will see the impact that poverty and inequality have on Niamh, who has found herself homeless in her native city of Dublin.

Niamh's story

'I would like to have a good job and to work and be independent. To be independent to support myself and whatever I need, like paying the rent and not having to depend on social welfare or anything like that.'

Niamh was homeless for six months before qualifying for rent allowance. She is only temporarily off the streets through the kindness of friends and is struggling to find somewhere to live.

'The landlords can't wait a few weeks for the rent and the deposit to come through; they want the money upfront. I don't have €800 to give them straight away,' she says.

Three years ago, Niamh completed a metalwork course and went looking for work, with little success. She found that there were few opportunities in the welding/metalwork field and employers were looking for people with advanced skills and more qualifications. She underwent further training to acquire computer and communication skills, but she still couldn't find a job.

Niamh struggled to overcome feelings of depression. With the support of Focus Ireland, she has returned to college to study fitness. She is also brushing up on job applications and her interview skills in the hope of better things to come.

The problem of finding somewhere to live, however, still haunts her.

'I was living in different hostels with about four people in the room and you can't really sleep. If somebody wakes up and makes noise or they come home late and they wake you up, then you can't say anything to them because you might get thrown out of the hostel. I live with my friend now but I have to move out soon because I don't want to destroy the relationship between me and my friend.'

Niamh lives on €144 a week and the recent cuts in rent allowance and **social welfare** just make everything that little bit harder.

'The way you live every day you have to sacrifice: your clothing, your food money and the rent. I'm still trying to move on and do my best', she says. 'I'm trying to save money to put in my account to have some money in case something happens but I can't save up the €800 or €900 for a deposit, so I am just hoping to find a landlord who can wait a few weeks until the rent comes through. Many of them don't accept rent allowance, so that is another problem.'

If the rules of rent allowance were changed to allow people to pay the deposit upfront to the landlord or if the landlord could wait a few weeks for the money to come through, Niamh says it would really help.

'We are in the middle and we are the ones who are suffering. We want to get a place as soon as we can, to go to work or to go to college, to do things,' she says. 'It affects us and you get depressed. Right now, since I don't have a place to live, I feel like I am just standing still. I can't move on.'

While there are supports to help people to return to education and training, which is useful, Niamh says: 'It is really all about jobs and job opportunities.' That is what she, like many others, is really looking for.

Source: Adapted from 'Now you see us: The human stories behind poverty in Ireland', Community Platform

Debate

- ⊘ Being Creative
- ⊘ Being Literate
- ⊘ Communicating
- ⊘ Managing Information and Thinking
- ⊘ Managing Myself
- ⊘ Working with Others

Organise a walking debate on the following topic:

 'Poverty in Ireland is a direct result of a lack of adequate housing.'

Having completed the debate, has your opinion remained the same or has it changed? Can you explain why?

Case study 2

This case study refers to poverty in parts of Greece. Greece used to be considered a resonably well-off country. It is a member state of the European Union and a popular destination for tourists. Unfortunately, due to the **financial crisis**, many people in Greece lost their jobs and their homes. The crisis was a trigger for poverty and inequality.

Poverty in Greece as a result of the economic crisis

A **humanitarian crisis** is unfolding in an **impoverished** Greek city where a deepening economic crisis has left thousands seeking food from an international charity. Once home to a thriving shipbuilding industry, the port city of Perama near Athens has seen its fortunes decrease over the years as buyers abandoned it for cheaper options outside Greece.

The country's financial crisis is the latest blow – pushing up unemployment in the area to 60%, triple the national average.

Without health insurance or money for fees at state facilities, many of the town's 25,000 residents have begun flocking to a free clinic set up by a charity organisation called Doctors of the World seeking medical care and, lately, staples like milk and bread.

The clinic was set up two years ago to treat poor immigrants. Instead, it now finds that 80% of its patients are Greeks struggling to get by.

'We tell a lot of people who come here: "Your child needs to go to the hospital, we can't treat the problem here," and they tell us: "I don't have the €1.40 to take the bus and go to the hospital",' said Liana Maili, a paediatrician at the clinic.

A large chunk of the town's residents live on less than two hundred euros a month, the agency says.

'There are some families that have not had electricity for five, eight months, who spent the winter burning pieces of wood to keep warm and whose children eat from the garbage.'

FOOD PARCELS

Greece is struggling through a debilitating debt crisis that has forced it to accept financial aid to keep afloat. Most Greeks have felt the pain of salary and pension cuts and higher taxes, with towns like Perama showing the extremes of a crisis that social workers say has punished the weakest people in society.

In the clinic's small waiting room, patients outnumber the available seats as they wait to be seen by a doctor or pick up a free meal box of beans, olive oil, pasta and condensed milk.

Unable to find a steady job for five years, Antonis Giatras relies on the clinic to feed his family of five. He recalls being forced to live in his car and in a cemetery for months when he and his pregnant wife were homeless.

'There are some days when we have no bread, or food,' said the fifty-year-old Giatras. 'My young daughter has to go to school some days without taking any food with her.'

In a one-room shack with a ceiling damaged by water and held together with bits of rope and wood, thirty-six-year-old Spiridoula Firlemi lives in fear her electricity will be cut off because she cannot pay back power bills of €1,250.

'They'll cut it off. We'll see, maybe I'll get electricity from a neighbour,' said Firlemi, who has a forty-five-day-old baby.

'I can't leave the baby in the cold.'

Source: Deborah Kyvrikosaios, Reuters, 30 March 2012

People waiting in line at a food bank

Doctors providing healthcare

Imagine!

- ⊘ Being Creative
- ⊘ Being Literate
- ⊘ Managing Information and Thinking
- ⊘ Managing Myself

Imagine that and your family has to survive on €200 per month. Describe the difficulties this would cause. In particular, refer to the items that your family may have to do without.

Take action!

- ⊘ Being Literate
- ⊘ Communicating
- ⊘ Managing Information and Thinking
- ⊘ Managing Myself
- ⊘ Working with Others

Invite a guest speaker from an organisation working to address problems of social inequality in Ireland to talk to your class group on the issues of poverty and inequality.

Don't forget to complete your reflections in your reflective journal.

Chapter 16

UNIT 4
LOCAL AND GLOBAL DEVELOPMENT

The causes of poverty

Learning outcomes

By the end of this chapter, having examined some of the causes of poverty, you should be able to form your own opinion on the reasons for poverty at home and abroad.

Key skills you will use in this chapter

- ✓ Being Creative
- ✓ Being Literate
- ✓ Being Numerate
- ✓ Communicating
- ✓ Managing Information and Thinking
- ✓ Managing Myself
- ✓ Staying Well
- ✓ Working with Others

Key words

- ⚷ Non-governmental organisations (NGOs)
- ⚷ Colonies
- ⚷ Legacy of colonialism
- ⚷ Colonialism
- ⚷ Civil war
- ⚷ National debt
- ⚷ Restructure
- ⚷ Infrastructure
- ⚷ Immunisation
- ⚷ Write-off
- ⚷ Gender discrimination
- ⚷ Natural disasters

Wellbeing indicators in this chapter

Governments, charity organisations, **non-governmental organisations (NGOs)** and individuals throughout the world have different views on the causes of poverty. It is difficult to point to one single reason why poverty exists in our world.

NGO working in a poverty-stricken area

While we all may have different opinions as to why poverty is such a problem, it is important that we examine the different reasons that may be at the heart of the problem. If we can understand the issues that cause poverty, then we may be able to tackle the problem more effectively.

We will examine some of the issues that cause poverty both locally and internationally. However, you may also be able to think of other issues that cause poverty. The following are some of the causes of poverty.

Video What is poverty?

History

Many of the poorest nations in the world used to be **colonies**. (A colony is a region that is under the control of another country and occupied by settlers from that country.) These colonies were slave-exporting areas and regions from which

resources have been taken and used to benefit colonial powers to make them richer. You may have learned about some of these examples in your history or geography classes.

For example, it is believed that the conquest of South America by Spain and Portugal has contributed to the problem of poverty in many parts of that continent. It is often referred to as the **legacy of colonialism**.

Colonial slave trade between Europe, Africa and South America

? Questions

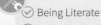

- Being Literate
- Managing Information and Thinking
- Managing Myself

1 Write down a list of five countries that you believe are suffering from poverty as result of colonialism.

2 Name three countries that used to be colonial powers.

War and political problems

In many countries where war and political problems exist, we can often trace the origins of the problems back to **colonialism**. In other countries, war and political problems may not result from colonialism. Regardless of the causes, it is clear that safety, stability and security are essential for a country to develop. Without these basics, it is impossible for a country to progress.

Likewise, laws are needed to protect people's rights, property and belongings. Political problems in certain countries mean laws are not enforced properly. Often it is the weaker members of society who suffer most as a result. When law and order breaks down, it can lead to **civil war** and people may become poor as a result. The poorest countries in the world all experienced civil war and serious political problems at some point in the twentieth century. Many of them have weak governments that cannot, or don't, protect people against violence.

The Democratic Republic of the Congo (formerly known as Zaire) was a colony. Ever since it became an independent country, it has been ravaged by war. It has had two major wars since independence. Almost 6 million people have been killed. It is one of the poorest countries in the world.

Democratic Republic of the Congo (DRC)

War and poverty are major problems in the DRC

The DRC has a beautiful landscape and varied wildlife

Research

Research the origins of war and political instability in the Democratic Republic of the Congo (DRC).

- Find out why this country has experienced such problems with war and political instability.
- How does poverty associated with war and political problems in the DRC affect day-to-day living?
- You can present your findings to your class in a digital format. For example, you can use PowerPoint, Movie Maker or any similar software or app.

- Being Creative
- Being Literate
- Communicating
- Managing Information and Thinking
- Managing Myself
- Working with Others

National debt

Many former colonies carry significant **national debt** due to loans from wealthier nations and international financial institutions. The problem for these countries is that for every $1 received in grant aid, they have to pay back an average of $2.30.

Read the following article.

Brazil to write off $900m of African debt

Brazil has said it plans to cancel or restructure $900 million worth of debt in 12 African countries, as part of a broader strategy to boost ties with the continent.

Brazilian officials said on Saturday that President Dilma Rousseff, visiting Ethiopian capital Addis Ababa to mark the African Union's 50th anniversary, was set to announce a new development agency alongside the cancellation that will offer assistance to African countries.

'The idea of having Africa as a special relationship for Brazil is strategic for Brazil's foreign policy,' Thomas Traumann, presidential spokesman, told reporters in Addis Ababa.

'Almost all (aid) is cancellation,' Traumann said.

Among the 12 countries whose debts were pardoned, Congo-Brazzaville was the highest with a $352 million debt cancelled, with Tanzania's $237 million debt the second largest.

Traumann said the move was part of Brazil's efforts to boost economic ties with Africa, home to some of the world's fastest-growing economies.

He added that Brazil recently established an agency to support investments in industry and development in Africa and Latin America.

SIGNING AGREEMENTS

Rousseff has met with several African leaders, including Ethiopian Prime Minister Hailemariam Desalegn, with whom she signed a series of co-operation agreements on agriculture, education, air transport and science.

Brazil's interest in Africa is part of a larger trend boosting so-called South–South Co-operation, which has attracted investment from emergent economies in developing countries, namely in Africa.

Brazil, one of five members of the BRICs emerging nations group and with a GDP of $2.425 trillion in 2012, is the world's seventh largest economy.

The BRICs countries – comprising Brazil, China, India and Russia – are now Africa's largest trading partners and its biggest new group of investors. BRICS–Africa trade is seen eclipsing $500 billion by 2015, according to Standard Bank.

Traumann said most of Brazil's future assistance would target infrastructure, agricultural and social programmes.

'Brazil has great expertise in what we call tropicalising European crops. We have that technology,' he said. 'The idea is how to transfer that technology from Brazil to other African countries.'

Source: Al Jazeera, 27 May 2013

The nations that grant these loans often insist on the poorer countries buying expensive products from them. This means that there is less money to invest in education, healthcare and jobs. Therefore, the poorer countries become poorer and get caught in a cycle of poverty. A cycle of poverty is when poverty keeps happening because the causes of poverty are not dealt with. Zambia is an example of such a country. Massive debt and interference from the people who gave Zambia loans meant large cuts were made in health and education. Many children did not receive **immunisation** because the government was too poor to provide the service.

One hope for countries experiencing poverty due to debt is if the people who give the loans agree to reduce or even **write off** (cancel completely) the debt.

Discrimination and social inequality

Poverty and inequality are two different things, but inequality can lead to poverty. For example, if people live in an area with few services, this can create an environment where poverty can flourish. If an area has minimal access to jobs, poverty can take hold.

Gender discrimination can also lead to poverty. In most societies, females are discriminated against. Women may receive very little pay for work done or may not be allowed to work. This means that women are often unable to provide for their families. The United Nations has declared that gender discrimination has been a significant factor in keeping many women and children around the world in poverty.

Zambia

Girl carrying rubbish on her head near Lusaka

Women working hard for little pay on the far side of the world

Women working hard for little pay closer to home

Vulnerability to natural disasters

Flooding in Bangladesh

Drought in the Sahel

In regions of the world that are already less wealthy, catastrophic **natural disasters** keep these regions in a constant state of poverty. The impact of flooding in Bangladesh, the drought in the Sahel region of Africa and the 2010 earthquake in Haiti show the havoc such devastation causes.

In each of these cases, people who were already poor became refugees within their own countries. They lost whatever little they had and were forced out of their homes, becoming almost completely dependent on others for survival.

Without assistance in the form of aid from other countries or organisations, governments in these countries would have been unable to meet the needs of their people.

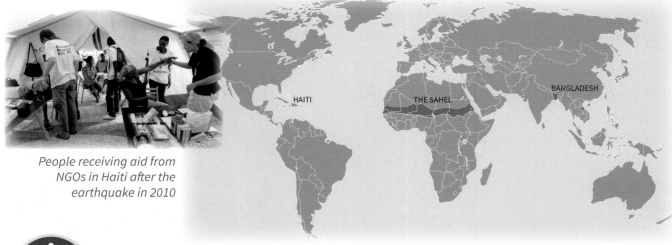

People receiving aid from NGOs in Haiti after the earthquake in 2010

HAITI THE SAHEL BANGLADESH

The location of Bangladesh, the Sahel region and Haiti

Take action!

- ✓ Being Literate
- ✓ Communicating
- ✓ Managing Information and Thinking
- ✓ Managing Myself
- ✓ Working with Others

Make contact with a governmental organisation or a non-governmental organisation, such as Irish Aid or Trócaire.

Ask if a guest speaker from one of these organisations could make a presentation to your class on the issue of natural disasters and poverty.

Don't forget to complete your reflections in your reflective journal.

Chapter 17

Local development

Learning outcomes

By the end of this chapter you should be able to identify some positive and negative effects of development in your locality.

Key words

🔑 Development 🔑 Revitalised
🔑 Redeveloped 🔑 Ghost estates

Wellbeing indicators in this chapter

Key skills you will use in this chapter

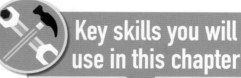

✓ Being Creative

✓ Being Literate

✓ Being Numerate

✓ Communicating

✓ Managing Information and Thinking

✓ Managing Myself

✓ Staying Well

✓ Working with Others

Development

When we examine our country, and indeed our local communities, we can see lots of evidence of development. In many cases, **development** in Ireland has been good for the country and its people. However, sometimes development can be negative for the country and for local communities.

Group activity

⊕ Divide the class into five groups. Each group should pick one of the photographs shown here. Each group should have a different photograph.

⊕ Examine the photograph with your group. Discuss whether your photograph represents a positive or a negative development. Your group must come up with three reasons for your decision. Report your ideas back to the class group.

- ☑ Being Literate
- ☑ Communicating
- ☑ Managing Information and Thinking
- ☑ Managing Myself
- ☑ Working with Others

Positive development

Grangegorman is located in Dublin 7, about 1.5 kilometres from the city centre. It was once home to a hospital, St Brendan's, but the area went into decline when the hospital was shut down. The land had much potential for development and is a great example of a planned development that is very positive for the area, and indeed, Dublin city.

This large site is being **redeveloped** on behalf of DIT and the HSE by an agency called the Grangegorman Development Agency (GGDA). It began work on the project in 2013 and, to date, huge progress has been made. Key aspects of the redevelopment so far include:

St Brendan's Hospital in Grangegorman

- 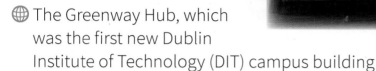 The Greenway Hub, which was the first new Dublin Institute of Technology (DIT) campus building

- A HSE primary care centre

- The new LUAS Cross-City line now stops at Grangegorman.

When it is finished, the redevelopment will have completely **revitalised** (brought new life to) the area. It will be a thriving community with access to both second-level and third-level education. It is a terrific example of how positive well-planned development can be.

An artist's impression of what the site will look like

An artist's impression of an aerial view of the complete site

 Imagine!

Imagine that you are a reporter for an online news journal. In your copybook, write a balanced report on how a development like Grangegorman influences a community.

A balanced report should refer to both positive and negative consequences.

 Being Creative
 Being Literate
⊘ Communicating
⊘ Managing Information and Thinking
⊘ Managing Myself

How development can have a negative effect on a local area

Ghost estates

During the Celtic Tiger period in Ireland, many housing estates were built in areas that did not have the services or transport facilities to match. The estates were often built by developers, some of whom were hoping to make a quick profit. Unfortunately, many of these estates were not completed because the developers ran out of money. In many communities, these unfinished estates, which came to be called **ghost estates**, fell into disrepair and became eyesores and health hazards.

Former ghost estates can have a positive effect. Renovating these estates could provide a possible solution to the problem of homelessness in Ireland.

Debate

- ⊘ Being Creative
- ⊘ Being Literate
- ⊘ Communicating
- ⊘ Managing Information and Thinking
- ⊘ Managing Myself
- ⊘ Working with Others

Organise a walking debate on the following topic:

 💬 'All recent developments in our community have been negative.'

Having completed the debate, has your opinion remained the same or has it changed? Can you explain why?

Take action!

- ⊘ Being Literate
- ⊘ Communicating
- ⊘ Managing Information and Thinking
- ⊘ Managing Myself
- ⊘ Working with Others

Your class could raise awareness about the positive and negative effects of development in your locality.

Organise a presentation to make to the school community outlining both positive and negative developments that have taken place in your locality. You could use photographic evidence or video evidence as part of your awareness campaign.

 Don't forget to complete your reflections in your reflective journal.

Chapter 18

UNIT 5
EFFECTING GLOBAL CHANGE

Power and influence

Learning outcomes

By the end of this chapter you will be able to identify people and institutions with power and influence in the world today.

Key skills you will use in this chapter

- ✓ Being Creative
- ✓ Being Literate
- ✓ Being Numerate
- ✓ Communicating
- ✓ Managing Information and Thinking
- ✓ Managing Myself
- ✓ Staying Well
- ✓ Working with Others

Key words

🔑 Constitution
🔑 Legislation
🔑 Veto

🔑 Budgetary matters
🔑 Sanctions
🔑 Trusteeship

Wellbeing indicators in this chapter

The European Parliament is an example of a powerful institution

147

Examine the following photographs showing powerful people in our world.

*Angela Merkel –
Chancellor of Germany*

*Vladimir Putin –
President of the Russian Federation*

*Christine Lagarde –
President of the European Central Bank*

*Xi Jinping – General Secretary of the
Communist Party of China*

*Jerome Powell –
Chair of the US Federal Reserve*

*António Guterres –
UN Secretary-General*

Let's examine another powerful role in some detail.

A powerful position: President of the United States of America

The White House, Washington, DC

Joe Biden is the 46th president of the United States

The US president is part of a larger system of government. There are three main branches of the US government:

The legislative branch makes laws

Senate
100 elected senators in total
2 senators per state
House of Representatives
435 representatives, representing the 50 states

The executive branch carries out laws

President
Vice-president
Cabinet
Nominated by the president and must be approved by the Senate (with at least 51 votes)

The judicial branch makes sure laws are fair

Supreme Court
9 justices nominated by the president and must be approved by the Senate (with at least 51 votes)
Other federal courts

The following are some of the powers that the American **constitution** gives the president:

🌐 Chief of state with the power to agree treaties with other states

🌐 Selects people to run the country

🌐 Commander-in-chief of the US military

🌐 Pardons people who have been convicted of crimes

🌐 Introduces and signs **legislation**.

The president has the power of **veto**. This means that the president can reject a decision made by a law-making body, such as Congress. Even though a majority of people want the bill to be made into law, the president can refuse to sign it into law.

Barack Obama was the US president from 2009 to 2017

The president is elected to serve a term of four years and may serve a maximum of two terms of office.

Barack Obama was elected president in 2008 and became the first African American president. There has yet to be a female president of the United States. This is in contrast to over sixty other nations. India's first woman leader came to power in 1966. In Argentina, it was 1974 and in Pakistan it was 1988.

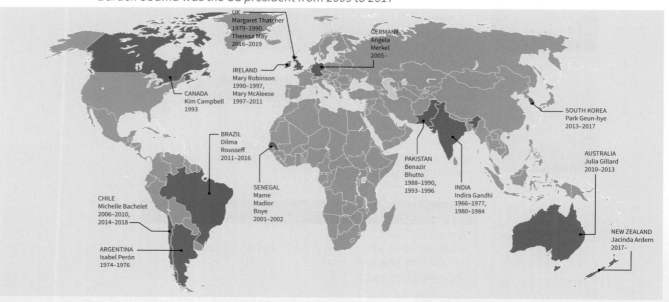

Some example of nations that have had female leaders

Debate

Organise a walking debate on the following topic:

 💬 'The next president of the United States of America should be a woman.'

When you have completed the debate, reflect on the arguments made in favour of and against the motion.

It is important to realise that people have differing perspectives on this issue. How did you feel about these differing views?

Did you change your mind at any time during the debate? Why?

- ✓ Being Creative
- ✓ Being Literate
- ✓ Communicating
- ✓ Managing Information and Thinking
- ✓ Managing Myself
- ✓ Working with Others

A powerful institution: The United Nations

The United Nations is an international organisation. It was founded in 1945 as a response to the terrible death and destruction caused by the First and Second World Wars. Its aim is to promote peace and security among all the states of the world.

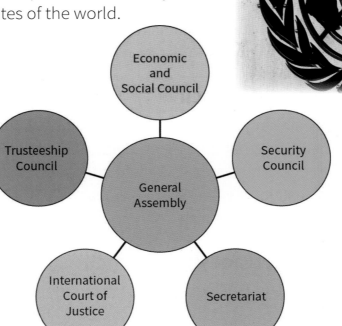

Structure of the United Nations

General Assembly

There are currently 193 member states that make up the General Assembly of the United Nations. In order to become a member, each state must be recommended by the United Nations Security Council.

General Assembly in session

Each year, in September, the full UN membership meets in the General Assembly Hall in New York for the annual General Assembly session and general debate, which many heads of state attend and address. Decisions on important questions, such as those on peace and security, admission of new members and **budgetary matters** (how finances are used) require a two-thirds majority of the General Assembly. Decisions on other questions are by simple majority. Each year, the General Assembly elects a General Assembly president to serve a one-year term of office.

Security Council

Under the UN Charter, the Security Council is responsible for international peace and security. It has fifteen members: five permanent and ten non-permanent members. Each member has one vote. Each member state must follow the Council's decisions. The Security Council monitors threats to peace around the world. When there is a threat to peace, it calls upon the parties to the dispute to settle it by peaceful means and recommends methods to sort out their differences. In some cases, the Security Council can impose **sanctions** (penalties) or even authorise the use of force to keep or restore international peace and security. The Security Council has a presidency, which changes every month.

Economic and Social Council

The Economic and Social Council monitors economic, social and environmental issues. It also implements international agreements and goals, such as development goals. It regularly sets goals to help improve people's lives, such as the United Nations Sustainable Development Goals. We will look at some of these goals in more detail later on in this strand.

South Sudan and surrounding countries

Trusteeship Council

The Trusteeship Council monitors territories that want to become independent states. It can take these territories under its control until a more permanent solution is found. Currently, there are no **trusteeships** (administration of a territory under UN supervision).

During the civil war in South Sudan (2013–2020) it was recommended that the region come under the trusteeship of the UN, since it was an unstable territory. However, the request was declined. In 2020 a peace deal was reached in the region.

International Court of Justice

The International Court of Justice is located in the Peace Palace in the Hague (Netherlands). The court's role is to settle, in accordance with international law, legal disputes submitted to it by states and to give advice on legal questions referred to it.

International Court of Justice

Secretariat

The Secretariat comprises the Secretary-General and tens of thousands of international UN staff members who carry out the day-to-day work of the UN. The secretary-general is the chief administrative officer of the organisation.

UN staff members are recruited internationally and locally. They work in duty stations and on peacekeeping missions all around the world. Serving the cause of peace can be a dangerous occupation. Since the founding of the United Nations, hundreds of brave men and women have given their lives in its service.

Irish troops in UN uniform

 Research

✓ Being Creative
✓ Being Literate
✓ Communicating
✓ Managing Information and Thinking
✓ Managing Myself
✓ Working with Others

Irish peacekeepers have worked in many dangerous situations and many have given their lives. In groups, research one of these missions and report your findings back to the class group.

 Imagine!

✓ Being Creative
✓ Being Literate
✓ Communicating
✓ Managing Information and Thinking
✓ Managing Myself
✓ Working with Others

Imagine that you are one of the influential people you've learned about. In your copybook, write down five key words you would use to show why you are powerful.

Group activity

The photographs show powerful European and international institutions. Divide the class into five groups. Each group will be assigned one photograph.

1 Write down the name of the institution represented by your photograph.

2 Research the role of that institution and the impact it has on the lives and wellbeing of citizens. Report your findings back to the class.

European Central Bank

United Nations headquarters

European Commission

International Criminal Court

International Monetary Fund headquarters

Take action!

You and your class group could research and develop a short account of the ten most influential people in the world today.

When you have completed this account, you could present your work for publication on your school's website.

Don't forget to complete your reflections in your reflective journal.

UNIT 5

EFFECTING GLOBAL CHANGE

An analysis of a global issue: Climate change

Learning outcomes

By the end of this chapter you will be able to assess the causes of climate change and the consequences of climate change. You will also understand how climate change impacts directly on people's lives. You will be able to suggest some possible solutions to the problem of climate change.

Key skills you will use in this chapter

- ✓ Being Creative
- ✓ Being Literate
- ✓ Being Numerate
- ✓ Communicating
- ✓ Managing Information and Thinking
- ✓ Managing Myself
- ✓ Staying Well
- ✓ Working with Others

Key words

- 🔑 Climate change
- 🔑 Climate change deniers
- 🔑 Intergovernmental Panel on Climate Change
- 🔑 Precipitation
- 🔑 Malaria
- 🔑 Parasite
- 🔑 Sub-Saharan Africa
- 🔑 Renewable sources

Wellbeing indicators in this chapter

A current global issue: Climate change

As we have seen, there are many issues and challenges facing the world in the twenty-first century. It is difficult to make the case for one being more important than any of the others. In your class group, people may have different ideas as to what is the most pressing challenge facing our planet today.

However, when we take a closer look at all of the challenges and issues we are facing, one of the most urgent problems affecting all humans in the world is that of **climate change**.

▶ **Video** Drop in the ocean? Ireland and climate change

What are the causes of climate change?

When we examined the concept of sustainability in Unit 3, we looked briefly at the topic of climate change. We will now examine the causes of climate change in more detail.

Life on Earth depends on energy coming from the sun. About half the light reaching the Earth's atmosphere passes through the air and clouds to the surface, where it is absorbed and then radiated back up in the form of infrared heat. About 90% of this heat is then absorbed by the greenhouse gases and radiated back towards the surface. This means that the Earth is warmed to an average of 15°C and that our planet is able to support life, and we can survive.

Unfortunately, this average temperature is beginning to increase. Most climate scientists agree that the main cause of the current global warming trend is the increase of the 'greenhouse effect' as a result of human activity.

Humans are releasing more and more gases such as nitrous oxide, carbon dioxide and methane into the atmosphere, which is increasing the greenhouse effect and driving up the Earth's average temperature. If you have ever been ill and had an increased temperature, you will know that it is dangerous. It is the same with our planet – increased temperatures are extremely dangerous.

On Earth, human activities are changing the natural greenhouse. Over the last century, burning fossil fuels like coal and oil has increased the amount of carbon dioxide (CO_2) in the atmosphere. This happens because the process of burning coal or oil combines carbon with oxygen in the air to make CO_2. Other ways that humans are adding to the problem is through industry and by clearing land for agriculture.

Some people strongly disagree that humans are the main cause of current climate change. These people are sometimes referred to as **climate change deniers**. They argue that the climate change that is currently happening is a natural phenomenon and not due to human activity. One argument put forward is that the sun is to blame for current global warming trends.

Emissions from vehicles

Emissions from industry

Emissions from livestock

As he sat in his livingroom, he pondered why everybody was so worried about climate change.

However, scientists have proven that the sun is not directly responsible for global warming. Since 1978, a series of satellite instruments has measured the energy output of the sun directly. The satellite results show a very slight drop in the amount of energy the sun has given off over this time period, so the sun doesn't appear to be responsible for global warming.

Intergovernmental Panel on Climate Change

The **Intergovernmental Panel on Climate Change**, a group of 1,300 independent scientific experts from countries all over the world, under the guidance of the United Nations, concluded that there is a more than 95% probability that human activities over the past fifty years have warmed our planet.

What are the consequences of climate change?

It is not easy to predict the consequences of climate change. However, scientists who report to the Intergovernmental Panel on Climate Change agree on the following:

🌐 On average, the Earth will become warmer. Some regions may experience warmer temperatures, but others may not.

Australia recorded its hottest year ever in 2019

🌐 Warmer conditions will probably lead to more evaporation and **precipitation** overall, but it will vary depending on the region. Some regions will become wetter and some will become drier.

Ireland has had extremely heavy rainfall in recent years

🌐 Climate change is intensifying. More droughts, storms and floods are taking place around the world.

🌐 A stronger greenhouse effect will cause the oceans to warm up. It also means that glaciers and polar ice caps will either partially or fully melt. This will result in sea levels rising, which will be devastating for many communities. It is estimated that 100 million people live just one metre above sea level.

Storm damage in the US

Flooding on a Pacific island

🌐 The water in the oceans will expand as it warms. This will also cause sea levels to rise. Rising seas can flood low-lying areas and islands, damage property and destroy ecosystems such as sand dunes and wetlands that protect coasts against storms. Some ocean species will become extinct as a result of the oceans warming up.

🌐 Some crops and other plants may grow faster and in greater quantities due to increased amounts of CO_2 in the atmosphere. They may also use water more efficiently.

🌐 Other crops may no longer be able to grow in certain regions. This could have a disastrous impact on the people who depend on these crops.

Melting ice caps

Rice in a paddy field

Crop failure in the Sahel

Impact of climate change on people's lives

Climate change will have some impact on the life of everyone living on this planet. Indeed, it may have an even bigger impact on those who have not yet been born.

Here are some of the recent consequences of climate change.

❶ Increase in natural disasters

It will cause an increase in both the number and ferocity of droughts, dust storms, floods, heatwaves, hurricanes, tornadoes and wildfires.

❷ Shortages of food and water

Climate change is making food production very difficult in some areas of the world. A lack of rainfall, which is a direct result of climate change, creates drought conditions. The soil dries up and plants such as maize and sorghum are unable to grow.

A maize crop

In 2017, drought in East Africa sent prices of basic food such as maize and sorghum soaring, according to the UN Food and Agriculture Organization (FAO). In Somalia, maize and sorghum harvests were estimated to be 75% lower than usual and more than half of the country's population, mostly in rural areas, was facing hunger.

Hunger can be a direct result of climate change

❸ Disease and climate change

▶ **Video** Malaria is spreading

There is a definite link between climate change and the spread of particular diseases, such as **malaria**. A person can contract malaria when bitten by a female mosquito that is infected with malaria. Carrying one of four parasites, it injects its saliva into the circulatory system and the **parasite** within travels to the liver, where it stays, matures and reproduces in large numbers.

The person will then experience symptoms such as severe headaches, fever, nausea, vomiting and chills. Without medical attention, it can result in serious illness and even death.

Malaria-carrying mosquitoes exist in **sub-Saharan Africa**, among other places. The climate there is ideal for the spread of malaria. Due to climate change, some species of malaria-carrying mosquitoes will be able to spread to regions that did not previously have malaria problems.

Malaria-infested regions such as Burkina Faso need to find solutions

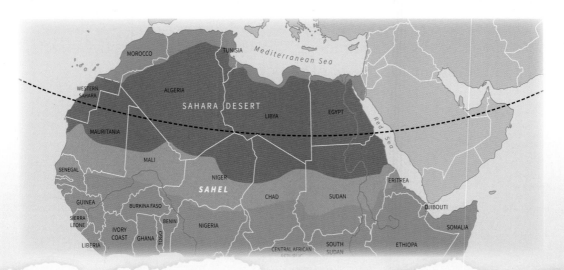

Sub-Saharan Africa

Are there solutions to the problem of climate change?

The Intergovernmental Panel on Climate Change has stated that if average temperatures increase by more than 2°C, it may be impossible to reverse the consequences of climate change. The challenge for our planet is to do everything we can to make sure temperatures don't increase any further.

The following are some ways in which we can reduce the impact of climate change:

🌐 Reduce and even eliminate fossil fuels as a source of energy. By doing this, we will reduce the level of dangerous greenhouse gases we are adding to the atmosphere.

🌐 Consume fewer products that we don't need. Many things we buy and consume are not necessary. Often they are packaged in a way that is environmentally unfriendly. By not consuming these, companies will produce less and won't release as many greenhouse gases.

🌐 Choose renewable sources of energy. We can choose to use energy created by **renewable sources** such as wind, solar or hydro.

🌐 Plant native trees in large numbers. This will have many positive effects, particularly in cleansing our air of carbon dioxide.

🌐 Encourage people to replace vehicles that run on petrol and diesel with electric vehicles. This change alone will dramatically help to reduce greenhouse emissions.

Research

Research three more possible solutions to climate change. Write them in your copybook.

- ✓ Being Creative
- ✓ Being Literate
- ✓ Managing Information and Thinking
- ✓ Managing Myself

Take action!

You can expand on the previous exercise on finding solutions in your local community to help to reduce the problem of climate change.

- ✓ Being Literate
- ✓ Communicating
- ✓ Managing Myself
- ✓ Working with Others

For example, you and your class could highlight steps that could be taken in your school to reduce amounts of water, energy or waste. You could then report your findings to the school's board of management and put forward your proposals for your school to help to reduce the impact of climate change.

 Don't forget to complete your reflections in your reflective journal.

Responsible consumption and production

Learning outcomes

By the end of this chapter you will have learned about a global challenge: the double problem of people consuming too much and also producing too much waste. You will be able to state some ways you can respond to this challenge.

Key words

- Consumption
- Production
- Overproduction
- Malnutrition
- Overconsumption
- Components
- Methane
- Degrade

Key skills you will use in this chapter

- ✓ Being Creative
- ✓ Being Literate
- ✓ Being Numerate
- ✓ Communicating
- ✓ Managing Information and Thinking
- ✓ Managing Myself
- ✓ Staying Well
- ✓ Working with Others

Wellbeing indicators in this chapter

The challenge: Responsible consumption and production

One of the United Nations Sutainable Development Goals is to encourage and develop responsible **consumption** and **production**.

Responsible Consumption and Production is Goal #12 of the United Nations Sustainable Development Goals

We are producing vast quantities of products that are putting a huge strain on the world's resources. The term **overproduction** is used to describe when we produce more of something than is necessary.

Here are some examples of how we are being irresponsible in the quantity of things we are producing:

🌐 We are producing more food globally than the world needs. This is incredible when we consider that so many people are suffering from hunger and **malnutrition**.

- ⊘ Being Creative
- ⊘ Being Literate
- ⊘ Communicating
- ⊘ Managing Information and Thinking
- ⊘ Managing Myself
- ⊘ Staying Well
- ⊘ Working with Others

Think, pair and share

The images here and on the previous page show examples of food waste. Think about ways in which you and your family could reduce waste in your everyday lives.

Turn to your partner. Listen to their ideas. With your partner, decide what ideas you would like to share with the class. Report your ideas back to the class group. Use the table in your reflective journal to write down your ideas.

Our **overconsumption** of resources is directly related to the overproduction of materials by a range of industries. For example, take a product such as a mobile phone. Millions of mobile phones are produced every year. Some people get a new phone and then replace it within a very short time for what is considered to be a better and more fashionable model.

Do we need these new models? Most of us don't *need* them, but we *desire* them because marketing campaigns by the manufacturers convince us that our lives will be improved by getting a new phone.

The important point to remember is the vast quantity of resources used and the waste generated to create these new models.

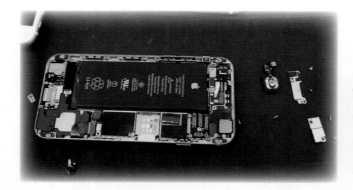

The photos above show some of the **components** used to make a modern mobile phone. To create each one of these components, valuable resources and energy (usually through the burning of fossil fuels) are required.

The question we need to ask is: can we justify the use of these resources and the pressure it puts on our planet? Are we overconsuming? What happens to the phones we no longer need? Are we creating unnecessary waste?

How to tackle overproduction and overconsumption

Eat less red meat

We get most of our red meat from livestock such as cattle and sheep. These animals produce **methane**, which is a greenhouse gas that has seventy-two times the impact of CO_2 over a twenty-year period. The emissions created by the meat an average family consumes equals the energy it takes to create a large 4X4 vehicle and the fuel it uses over five years!

There is no need to cut out red meat entirely, but eating fewer steaks and burgers means far less production of red meat and lower emissions.

Avoid buying plastic water bottles

Millions of plastic water bottles are bought every day. These plastics greatly damage our environment. As we have previously learned, it can take up to 450 years for these bottles to **degrade**. It also requires a lot of energy to create them. We can have a genuine impact on reducing consumption and waste if we choose not to purchase these bottles.

Break the link between consumption and happiness

One of the most important things we need to do is to break the link between consumption and happiness. Billions of euro are spent by large multinational companies to persuade us that we need certain products in order to be happy. We need to understand that happiness is not related to having lots of 'stuff'. When we realise this, we will be happier and also consume less, which in turn will help the planet to heal.

Research

- ⊘ Being Creative
- ⊘ Being Literate
- ⊘ Being Numerate
- ⊘ Communicating
- ⊘ Managing Information and Thinking
- ⊘ Managing Myself
- ⊘ Staying Well
- ⊘ Working with Others

Research a product or resource that you think is creating a problem in relation to overproduction and/or overconsumption. Present the following findings to your class:

- ❯ Name the problem.
- ❯ Is it a result of overproduction, overconsumption or both?
- ❯ Describe why you think it is a problem.
- ❯ What is the main cause of this problem?
- ❯ Who or what is most responsible for this problem?
- ❯ Can you supply facts or figures to support your argument?
- ❯ What solution can you come up with to help reduce this problem?
- ❯ Why, do you think, would this solution work?

Report back to your class in a digital format. You could use PowerPoint, Movie Maker or any other similar software or app.

Take action!

- ⊘ Being Literate
- ⊘ Communicating
- ⊘ Managing Information and Thinking
- ⊘ Managing Myself
- ⊘ Working with Others

You and your class group could write, direct and film a short video showing how teenagers can break the link between consumption and happiness.

You could ask for permission to link the video to your school's website as a resource for you school's Wellbeing programme.

Don't forget to complete your reflections in your reflective journal.

A campaign for change

Learning outcomes

By the end of this chapter you will have examined a sustainable campaign for change. You will have assessed how successful the campaign was. You will also understand the reasons why that campaign was successful or not.

Key words

- Millennium Development Goals
- Global partnership
- Eradicate
- Sustainable Development Goals

Key skills you will use in this chapter

- ✓ Being Creative
- ✓ Being Literate
- ✓ Being Numerate
- ✓ Communicating
- ✓ Managing Information and Thinking
- ✓ Managing Myself
- ✓ Staying Well
- ✓ Working with Others

Wellbeing indicator in this chapter

A campaign for change

The United Nations has set **Millennium Development Goals** for the twenty-first century. In this chapter we will examine one of these goals and whether or not this campaign has been successful. We will examine Goal #1, which is to eradicate extreme poverty and hunger.

In September 2000, world leaders came together at the United Nations headquarters in New York to adopt the United Nations Millennium Declaration. The world leaders committed their nations to a new **global partnership** to reduce extreme poverty. For the first time ever, they set targets, with a deadline of 2015, that became known as the Millennium Development Goals.

Speaking in 2012, the then Secretary-General of the United Nations, Ban Ki-moon, said:

'Eradicating extreme poverty continues to be one of the main challenges of our time, and is a major concern of the international community. Ending this scourge will require the combined efforts of all, governments, civil society organisations and the private sector, in the context of a stronger and more effective global partnership for development. The Millennium Development Goals set time-bound targets, by which progress in reducing income poverty, hunger, disease, lack of adequate shelter and exclusion — while promoting gender equality, health, education and environmental sustainability — can be measured. They also embody basic human rights — the rights of each person on the planet to health, education, shelter and security. The Goals are ambitious but feasible and, together with the comprehensive United Nations development agenda, set the course for the world's efforts to alleviate extreme poverty by 2015.'

The focus of this goal seems simple. The campaign hoped to end hunger worldwide by ensuring that every person had access to a safe supply of nutritious food. Specific targets were set.

Targets

> Between 1990 and 2015, halve the proportion of people whose income is less than $1 a day.

> Achieve full and productive employment and decent work for all, including women and young people.

> Between 1990 and 2015, halve the proportion of people who suffer from hunger.

Let's look at the outcomes of this campaign. How successful has it been?

On 25 September 2013, the president of the UN General Assembly hosted a special event to follow up on efforts made towards achieving the Millennium Development Goals. It seemed that while great progress had been made in relation to the goals, much more work needed to be done.

In relation to the three targets set out to eradicate hunger, the following results were revealed in 2013:

Results

> The proportion of people living in extreme poverty declined by half at the global level.

> In developing regions, the percentage of people living on less than $1.25 a day fell from 47% in 1990 to 22% in 2010, five years ahead of schedule.

> While the percentage of undernourished people globally decreased from 23.2% in 1990–1992 to 14.9% in 2010–2012, this still left 870 million people – one in eight worldwide – going hungry.

The campaign to **eradicate** hunger was successful in many ways. The problem was reduced dramatically in developing countries. However, the United Nations felt that a new campaign was needed to increase efforts, with the aim of ending hunger on the planet.

Here are some reasons why the campaign to eradicate extreme poverty and hunger was not a total success.

 The goal may not have been achievable in such a short space of time.

Governments did not make enough of a financial commitment to tackle the problem.

The financial crisis took the focus away from the problems of the developing world.

Debate

- ⊘ Being Creative
- ⊘ Being Literate
- ⊘ Communicating
- ⊘ Managing Information and Thinking
- ⊘ Managing Myself
- ⊘ Working with Others

Organise a walking debate on the following topic:

💬 'The United Nations campaign to eradicate hunger and poverty will never be achieved.'

When you have finished the debate, reflect on whether your opinion has remained the same or has changed. What do you think has changed your mind (if it has changed)? Or has your opinion remained the same?

In 2015, countries adopted the 2030 Agenda for Sustainable Development and its seventeen **Sustainable Development Goals**.

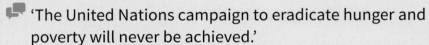

As you can see, the goal to eradicate hunger is still an important target for the United Nations. It is now Goal #2 in the new campaign. The official title of Goal #2 is: End hunger, achieve food security and improved nutrition and promote sustainable agriculture.

Once again, targets have been set to end hunger worldwide. The deadline for these targets is 2030. Here are some of the new targets that have been set to achieve the goal:

New targets

By 2030, end hunger and ensure access by all people, in particular the poor and people in vulnerable situations, including infants, to safe, nutritious and sufficient food all year round.

By 2030, double the agricultural productivity and incomes of small-scale food producers.

By 2030, end all forms of malnutrition.

Correct and prevent **trade restrictions**. This means that farmers in developing countries can sell their produce at a fair price.

Connect and communicate

You can become actively involved in this new campaign for change.

The United Nations wants you to commit to helping to end hunger. Go to the official UN Zero Hunger Challenge website and find out what you can do to help achieve this goal.

- ✓ Being Literate
- ✓ Communicating
- ✓ Managing Information and Thinking
- ✓ Managing Myself
- ✓ Staying Well
- ✓ Working with Others

Don't forget to complete your reflections in your reflective journal.

Sample citizenship action: Raising awareness of electricity conservation in school

Our teacher told us about using solar panels as one way of reducing energy consumption in our school

Our class had been learning about the idea of sustainability. We had examined our ecological footprints and were shocked at how high each student's footprint was. We all wanted to try to reduce our ecological footprint in some way. After consulting with our CSPE teacher, we decided that we would try to encourage all members of the school community to reduce their ecological footprints.

Our teacher organised a brainstorming session so that we could discuss some practical ways in which all members of the school community could be encouraged to reduce their ecological footprint. We decided to have an awareness-raising campaign about reducing electricity consumption in school.

Our teacher organised the class into different committees. Each committee had a specific responsibility and each member of the committee had a specific role to play.

One committee gathered as much information as possible from the principal and school board of management in relation to the amount of electricity being consumed in the school and the cost of this.

Another committee wrote to the Sustainable Energy Authority of Ireland asking for some practical solutions for reducing energy consumption in the school.

A third committee undertook a survey of classrooms and offices in the school to see if there were any obvious areas where energy consumption could be reduced.

The fourth committee analysed the information from the survey and came up with suggestions that could be easily implemented.

These suggestions were then brought to another committee. This committee was responsible for coming up with a strategy for raising awareness of the ways in which we could all reduce the school's energy consumption.

One very simple solution was to ask all teachers to ensure that all computers were shut down at the end of each school day. Shutting down all computers saves the school huge sums of money and greatly reduces energy consumption.

A publicity committee was responsible for communicating the information to all members of the school community. The information was posted on the school's website and they also created posters outlining the practical ways in which people could reduce energy consumption in the school. These were put in each classroom to remind people of their role in reducing consumption.

The awareness-raising campaign was a huge success. Over the course of one school year, consumption rates for energy decreased dramatically. The school's board of management was delighted with the campaign and has decided to explore other ways of reducing energy consumption in the school.

The campaign contributed greatly to the overall wellbeing of the school community.

Strand 2: Suggested actions

Now take action to enhance your learning.

The following are suggested actions that are linked mainly to Strand 2.

 Create a wellbeing mural or noticeboard, highlighting the link between the wellbeing of people and the planet.

 Organise a class debate on a local or global development issue.

 Research case studies to find out how Ireland's official development assistance (ODA) is tackling poverty and inequalities in specific countries.

 Write a letter or email to a politician or media outlet about a local or global issue of concern.

 Measure the attempts of your class to lessen your collective impact on the planet over an agreed period. Calculate your combined ecological footprint before and after you take action.

 Investigate the use of art, comedy, drama, poetry, music or multimedia to communicate how to address the challenge of climate change.

 Organise a pop-up fashion swap-shop to recycle clothing and raise awareness about sustainable consumption and production.

 Invite a guest speaker(s) to talk to your class/school about a local or global development issue of interest/concern.

 Make a visit to an organisation or community focused on sustainability issues.

 Support the work of a non-governmental organisation that addresses local or global inequalities. Help their efforts for campaigning, raising awareness or fundraising.

STRAND 3

EXPLORING DEMOCRACY

In this strand you will examine the meaning of democracy and how it works. You will examine the law and how citizens interact with it. You will also explore the role of the media in a democracy.

Unit 6   THE MEANING OF DEMOCRACY

Democracy is a system of government where citizens exercise power directly or elect people to represent them.

Unit 7   THE LAW AND THE CITIZEN

In this unit you will examine how laws are made and enforced. You will also learn how the law impacts on citizens and how citizens can bring about change in the law.

Unit 8   THE ROLE OF THE MEDIA IN A DEMOCRACY

This unit focuses on the role of different types of media in a democratic society. You will also learn about the increasing role of digital media in modern society.

The impact democracy has on your everyday life

Learning outcomes

By the end of this chapter you will understand the impact democracy has on your everyday life. You will be able to create a visual representation of the day-to-day contexts and institutions to which you belong, highlighting where you have power and influence.

Key skills you will use in this chapter

- ✓ Being Creative
- ✓ Being Literate
- ✓ Being Numerate
- ✓ Communicating
- ✓ Managing Information and Thinking
- ✓ Managing Myself
- ✓ Staying Well
- ✓ Working with Others

Key words

- ⚷ Direct democracy
- ⚷ Representative democracy
- ⚷ Social standing
- ⚷ Freedom of expression
- ⚷ Petition
- ⚷ Lobbying
- ⚷ Majority rule
- ⚷ Minority rights
- ⚷ Civic participation
- ⚷ Globalisation

Wellbeing indicators in this chapter

What is democracy?

Democracy is a form of government and it is the way that Ireland is run. The word *democracy* comes from two Greek words: *demos*, which means 'people', and *kratina*, which means 'to rule'. Put simply, democracy means 'rule by the people'. Power is in the hands of the people because it is they who elect the people to run the country on their behalf.

The birth of democracy can be traced back to Ancient Greece. Athens, which was a state in Greece at that time, was ruled by a **direct democracy**. This meant that citizens had a direct say in how the state was run. This was possible because Athens had a small population then. All the citizens met in an assembly and made their views known. However, to be considered a citizen of Athens, you had to be male and own property, and you had to have been born in Athens. Women and slaves, as well as people who were not born in Athens, were not considered to be citizens and had no say in the running of the state.

US President Abraham Lincoln (1809–1865) described democracy as:

'Government of the people, by the people, for the people.'

In Ireland we are governed by **representative democracy**. The population of the Republic of Ireland is almost 5 million people. It would be impossible for all of our citizens to have a direct say in the affairs of the state, so we elect representatives to run the state on our behalf. Citizens hold elections to choose their representatives. Every citizen over the age of eighteen who is resident in Ireland can vote in these elections.

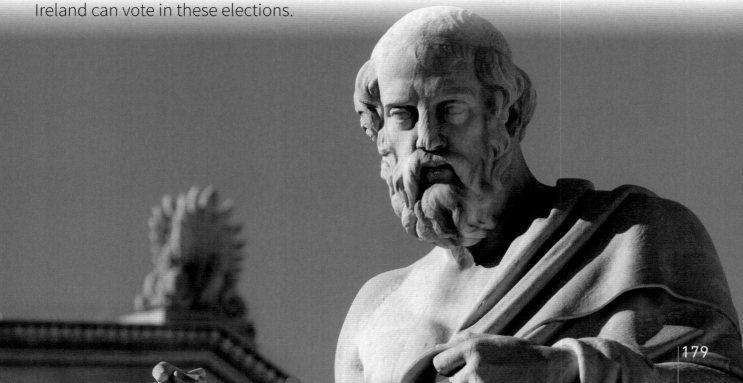

What influence does democracy have on my life?

Living in a democratic state, you have certain rights and freedoms. Unlike states where democracy is not practised, you are entitled to these rights and freedoms, regardless of your age, religion or whether you are male or female.

You have the following rights and freedoms

1 The right to be treated equally, regardless of gender, colour, race or social standing

Every single American – gay, straight, lesbian, bisexual, transgender – every single American deserves to be treated equally in the eyes of the law and in the eyes of our society.
– Barack Obama

2 The right to freedom of expression

Freedom of expression entitles you to express your opinion and to take part in debates. Individuals are also entitled to express their opinions through the media by means of television, newspapers, radio and social media. This is called freedom of the press.

3 The right to criticise the government if you don't agree with its policies or laws

You may do this by organising or participating in a protest, signing a **petition** or **lobbying** the government.

PETITION FORM

the undersigned, are concerned citize...ho urge ou...

4 The right to vote in elections

5 The right to run for election

6 The right to equality before the law

7 The freedom to practise your religion

8 The freedom to set up or join associations, organisations, political parties or trade unions

Democracy is also based on the principle of **majority rule** and **minority rights**. This means that decisions are made on the basis of majority agreement (opting for the decision most of the people agree with), with the knowledge that the rights and freedoms of those in the minority must be respected. The voice of the minority is listened to. In addition, democracies generally have a number of political parties, each with its own views on how the country should be run.

How does democracy influence my life on a daily basis?

"If this family is a democracy, why can't I run for Father?"

1 Democracy at home

2 Democracy in school

3 Democracy in institutions and organisations in your local community

Think, pair and share

Think about how these images of democracy influence you in your day-to-day life.

Share your ideas with your partner, then report your findings to the class group. Use the table in your reflective journal to write down your ideas.

- ⊘ Being Creative
- ⊘ Being Literate
- ⊘ Communicating
- ⊘ Managing Information and Thinking
- ⊘ Managing Myself
- ⊘ Working with Others

Create a video

Following on from your think, pair and share exercise, create a visual presentation of the organisations and groups you belong to and how they represent democracy in your daily life. You can create a short video or vlog for presentation to your class.

- ⊘ Being Literate
- ⊘ Managing Information and Thinking
- ⊘ Managing Myself
- ⊘ Working with Others

What power do I have to influence democracy?

One way of increasing your democratic voice is to seek a reduction of the voting age. Irish citizens who are resident in Ireland have the right to vote when they reach eighteen years of age. Other countries allow people to vote at a younger age.

What do you think of this? Do you feel strongly about it? Read the following letter sent to a national newspaper by a local representative. The writer believes that the voting age should be reduced to sixteen in Ireland. This is a good example of using your freedom of expression.

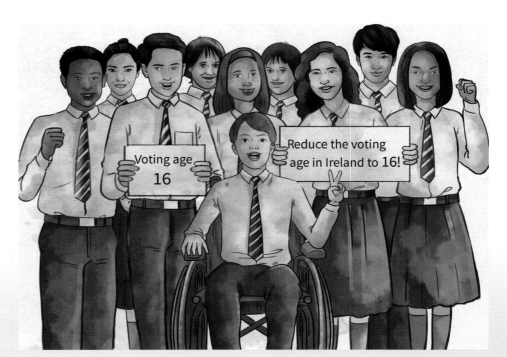

Reducing the voting age

To whom it may concern,

I find it astonishing that Government is not proceeding with a referendum to reduce the voting age to sixteen. We would do well to look to Scotland and Brazil where sixteen- and seventeen-year-olds were allowed to vote in recent elections.

If we followed their example, it would lead to great **civic participation**. An Austrian election study found that those who vote at a younger age tend to keep voting as they get older. Despite what some would have you believe, young people are interested in politics. Issues such as **globalisation**, the cost of college, the environment, car insurance are some of the issues that matter to them.

When will the establishment wake up and pay attention to the views and concerns of young people? By lowering the voting age, I suspect this would happen quite quickly.

Yours in optimism,

Cllr D.V. O' Brien,
Cavan County Council

 ## Questions

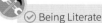
- Being Literate
- Managing Information and Thinking
- Managing Myself

1 What, do you think, is meant by the term 'referendum' in the letter?

2 According to the letter writer, why would it be more practical for people to be allowed to vote for the first time at age sixteen rather than age eighteen?

 ## Take action!

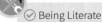
- Being Literate
- Communicating
- Managing Information and Thinking
- Managing Myself
- Working with Others

Use your power and influence to promote democracy!

You and your class could organise a petition asking your local representative to draft a bill that would reduce the voting age in Ireland to sixteen. Your petition should focus on the issue of democracy and how reducing the voting age will give young people a more democratic voice. The Change.org website has a useful tool for creating online petitions.

 Don't forget to complete your reflections in your reflective journal.

How democracy works in your school community

Learning outcomes

By the end of this chapter you should be able to describe some of the decision-making processes and the roles of different groups in your class or school.

Key words

- Democratic community
- Democratic process
- Rights
- Responsibilities
- Legislation
- Student council
- Parents' council
- Patron
- Trustees
- Ethos
- Board of management

Key skills you will use in this chapter

- ✓ Being Creative
- ✓ Being Literate
- ✓ Being Numerate
- ✓ Communicating
- ✓ Managing Information and Thinking
- ✓ Managing Myself
- ✓ Staying Well
- ✓ Working with Others

Wellbeing indicators in this chapter

You can see democracy in action in many of the communities to which you belong. A **democratic community** is one in which everyone is given the right to participate, make decisions or elect people.

Your class group and school community are examples of democracy in action. Decisions are made on a regular basis that affect your life in school. We will now look at how these decisions are made and the roles played by different people and groups in these decisions.

Classroom democracy

As a student you are a member of a class group. Class groups work most effectively when they are part of a **democratic process**.

Democratically run class groups are based on **rights** and **responsibilities**. (Remember, you learned about rights and responsibilities in Strand 1 of this book.) Members have certain rights but also have specific

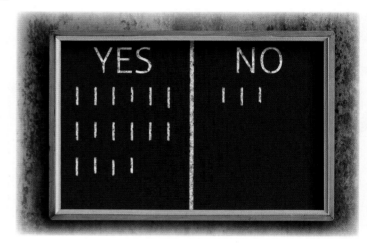

responsibilities attached to these rights. In the following activity, you and your class group will use the democratic process to develop a system that will help your class group.

Think, pair and share

- ⊘ Being Creative
- ⊘ Being Literate
- ⊘ Communicating
- ⊘ Managing Information and Thinking
- ⊘ Managing Myself
- ⊘ Staying Well
- ⊘ Working with Others

Think about some class rules that are important to the wellbeing of your class group.

Share your thoughts with your partner, then come up with a list of the class rules on which you both agree. (This is democracy in action!)

Share your views with the class group. The class group should then come up with a list of class rules that everyone agrees on. (Democracy in action again!) Use the table in your reflective journal to write down your ideas.

School democracy

Schools should be run democratically, but this has not always been the case. Indeed, there are parts of the world where schools are not democratically run.

Under **legislation** in Ireland (Education Act, 1998), schools are required to give a voice to every member of the school community. Schools have large numbers of people involved at different levels, so it makes sense that they need different groups to represent these large numbers.

In most second-level schools, the following groups are represented.

The student council

Schools should have an active **student council** in place. A student council can ensure that all students are represented. The student council has a vital role to play in expressing the views of students to the school management. It also has an important role to play in developing and reviewing school policies for the benefit of the school community. The student council should act as a voice for all students.

The parents' council

The **parents' council** aims to support the parents and guardians of students. In most schools there is a democratically elected parents' council. The parents' council also has a role in developing and reviewing school policy.

Teaching staff representatives

Teaching staff in schools are represented by members of staff who are democratically elected to the board of management. Their role is to represent members of the teaching staff and to help develop and review school policies.

The school's patron or trustee

The **patron** (owner) or **trustee** (people with the overall responsibility) of a school is the person or organisation that sets up the school. It may be a religious order, a bishop, an Education and Training Board, an organisation such as Educate Together or a combination of two of these. The patron/trustee will decide the **ethos** (guiding beliefs) of the school.

All of the above groups, except the student council, will provide representatives to the board of management. The **board of management** manages the school on behalf of the patron/trustees and must be accountable to both the patron and the Minister for Education and Skills.

Take action!

⊘ Being Literate
⊘ Communicating
⊘ Managing Information and Thinking
⊘ Managing Myself
⊘ Working with Others

Invite a guest speaker from the parents' council in your school to talk to your class about the role that the parents' council plays in the decision-making process in your school.

Don't forget to complete your reflections in your reflective journal.

Systems of government

Learning outcomes

By the end of this chapter you will understand some different systems of government. You will be able to compare two or more systems of government. You will understand how the state interacts with its citizens and how citizens can shape the state.

Key skills you will use in this chapter

- ✓ Being Creative
- ✓ Being Literate
- ✓ Being Numerate
- ✓ Communicating
- ✓ Managing Information and Thinking
- ✓ Managing Myself
- ✓ Staying Well
- ✓ Working with Others

Key words

- Government
- Constitution
- Elections
- Parliamentary democracy
- TDs
- General election
- Opposition
- Absolute monarchy
- Constitutional monarchy
- One-party state
- Dictators
- Dictatorship

Wellbeing indicator in this chapter

What is government?

Every day we hear about the decisions and actions of governments throughout the world. What do we mean when we talk about government?

Government can refer to an individual or a group of people who rule and manage the affairs of a country. Governments are very powerful because they have the authority to make important decisions on behalf of the people. Different systems of government exist. The system of government determines how the country is run and how it interacts with its citizens.

Think, pair and share

- ⊘ Being Creative
- ⊘ Being Literate
- ⊘ Communicating
- ⊘ Managing Information and Thinking
- ⊘ Managing Myself
- ⊘ Working with Others

Think about your understanding of government and the role it plays in society.

Write down your definition of government. Now turn to your partner. What is their definition of government? Decide on the definition you would like to share with the class group. Use the table in your reflective journal to help you.

Systems of government

There are many systems of government throughout the world. The map below highlights some countries that employ different systems of government.

Legend:
- Democracy
- Absolute monarchy
- Constitutional monarchy
- One-party state
- Dictatorship

Note: The map highlights selected countries as examples. The countries shown in dark green employ various different systems of government.

Questions

1 What country on the map has a one-party state? (Use your atlas to help you!)

2 Name three forms of government evident in Europe.

3 Name one country that is an absolute monarchy.

4 What is the system of government in the United Kingdom?

- ⊘ Being Literate
- ⊘ Managing Information and Thinking
- ⊘ Managing Myself

Democratic governments

Most countries today are democracies. Most democracies have a **constitution**. This is a written document that outlines how the country is run, the basic laws of the country and the rights and freedoms of its citizens. A constitution is important because it protects the rights of citizens and it ensures that the government doesn't have too much power.

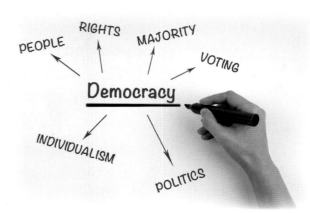

People vote for political candidates in **elections**. Citizens have the right to participate in civic and political society and are encouraged to get involved in the decision-making process at both local and national level. Citizens also have the right to question and criticise the government if they disagree with its actions. If citizens are unhappy with a government, they can vote the members out. Citizens have the right to protest against government decisions.

The rights and freedoms of citizens in countries with democratic systems of government mean that the people have a lot of power. Citizens have a say in decisions that affect them. This enables citizens to influence the government and shape the state as they see fit.

Different countries exercise democracy in different ways. Ireland, for example, is a **parliamentary democracy**. The parliament (Dáil Éireann) makes decisions and laws on behalf of its citizens. Citizens have the power to elect members to parliament. Members of parliament in Dáil Éireann are called **TDs**. The government is formed by the political party that wins the most seats in a **general election**.

One of the main features of a parliamentary democracy is the role of opposition parties. The **opposition** comprises the political parties or TDs that are not in government. The main role of opposition parties is to challenge the government if they feel its decisions, policies or laws are unfair or unjust. This ensures that the government is accountable and doesn't abuse its power.

If citizens are unhappy with the government, they have the power to vote for different people in the next general election. This ensures that the power remains in the hands of citizens.

Other democratic systems of government include presidential republics and presidential parliamentary governments.

Non-democratic governments

Not all countries have democratic systems of government. Some countries have non-democratic systems of government. In comparison to democracies, these systems interact a lot differently with their citizens. Let's explore these systems of government.

Absolute monarchies

A monarchy exists when a king, queen or members of a royal family rule a country. An **absolute monarchy** exists when a king or queen's rule is absolute. This means that they have the absolute power to make decisions or pass laws.

Absolute monarchs are not only the head of state, but they are also the head of the government. They are not answerable to a parliament or its citizens, nor do they have to consult with others if they want to introduce a new law. This means that the monarch can pass any laws they want, even if those laws infringe on the rights of the citizens.

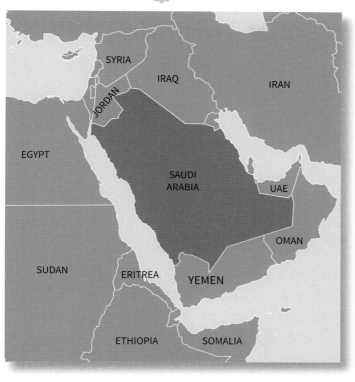

Absolute monarchs therefore have a lot of power. Unlike democratic systems of government, citizens have very little power and have little scope to influence how the country is run. In this system of government, there are no political parties and no opposition to the government. This means that the government cannot be challenged or criticised. Citizens have no power to elect their government since power is passed along the family line. There are few opportunities for citizens to participate in political life. Citizens are often viewed as subjects who must serve the ruler. As a result, few citizens challenge or question the government and many citizens feel powerless.

Saudi Arabia is an example of a country that is ruled by an absolute monarch. Saudi Arabia is currently ruled by King Salman. Some human rights organisations are critical of the strict regime in Saudi Arabia. Some argue that the Saudi rule denies citizens their rights. For example, until recently women were not allowed to drive a car or attend a football match. Freedom of expression is also limited. Many journalists and political commentators have been jailed because they have criticised the government.

King Salman of Saudi Arabia is an absolute monarch

Queen Elizabeth II is the head of state of a constitutional monarchy

Constitutional monarchies

Absolute monarchies should not be confused with **constitutional monarchies**. Constitutional monarchies exist when a king or queen is the head of state. Unlike absolute monarchies, however, these monarchs have limited powers because they are bound by a constitution. In addition, there is usually a parliamentary system whereby a prime minister is elected by the people. The prime minister and the government have the power to rule and make decisions on behalf of the citizens. Citizens in these countries have the same rights and freedoms as those with democratic systems of government. The UK is an example of a constitutional monarchy.

One-party states

In this system of government, only one political party has the right to form the government. Therefore, only one political party exists. Sometimes other political parties are forbidden. As a result, there is little or no opposition to challenge the government. Freedom of expression is limited and many citizens feel powerless to criticise the government and its policies. Some argue that one-party states limit the rights of citizens. Citizens don't have the same rights and freedoms as citizens living in democratic states. The government is rarely accountable and there are no checks and balances to prevent the abuse of power.

One example of a **one-party state** is the People's Republic of China. The most powerful political party is the Communist Party of China. It has been the most powerful party since 1949. This party holds the monopoly on representing the whole of Chinese society.

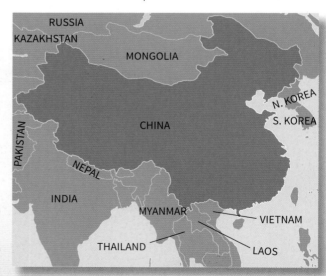

Dictatorships

Some countries are ruled by **dictators**. A state ruled by a dictator is called a **dictatorship**. Dictators are leaders who hold absolute power. This means that only the dictator has the power to make decisions, manage the affairs of the country and make new laws on behalf of the citizens.

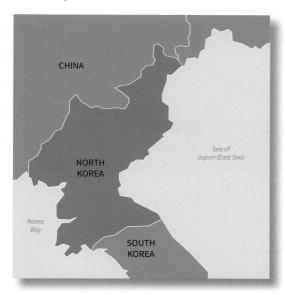

Dictators are very powerful leaders. To maintain power, dictators often ban political parties. In the eyes of a dictator, an alternative political party would weaken their position. As a result, there are usually no elections. This limits citizens' rights to elect or influence the government. There is little scope for citizens to shape the state. Any attempt to challenge the power of the dictator is suppressed, sometimes violently. This is because dictators often control the police force and the military too.

Citizens living under dictatorships often have their rights denied. Those who speak out against the government or leader are often arrested and imprisoned. Freedom of expression is frowned upon.

There are numerous dictatorships in the world today, located in Africa, South America, Asia and the Middle East. One of the most recognisable dictators is Kim Jong-un, President of North Korea and Supreme Commander of the North Korean Army.

Kim Jong-un

Citizens in North Korea don't have the freedom to travel and many find it difficult to leave the country. Television, news and media are under government control. As a result, citizens don't have access to information and don't know what is going on in the world around them. It is estimated that there are over 100,000 prisoners in North Korean prisons accused of political crimes.

Citizens in North Korea are constantly reminded of the power of their leader. Giant murals and statues of their leader adorn the main cities in North Korea. This reminds citizens that they have very little power to shape their country and that the power of their leader is absolute.

Individual activity

- Being Literate
- Managing Information and Thinking
- Managing Myself

Think about how democratic and non-democratic systems of government interact with their citizens. Copy the table below to your copybook, then fill it in to highlight the main differences between these systems of government in terms of:

- Power
- The rights of citizens
- Citizens' ability to influence the government and shape the state.

Factor	Democratic systems of government	Non-democratic systems of government
Power		
The rights of citizens		
Citizens' ability to influence the government and shape the state		

Take action!

- Being Creative
- Being Literate
- Communicating
- Managing Information and Thinking
- Managing Myself
- Working with Others

Create a PowerPoint presentation about systems of government in the world today. Present your findings to other students in your class or school.

Don't forget to complete your reflections in your reflective journal.

Irish democratic institutions

Learning outcomes

By the end of this chapter you will gain an understanding of some of the institutions that help democracy work in Ireland. You will be able to describe democratic structures for decision-making at local and national government levels. You will be familiar with the terminology associated with democracy in the Irish state.

Key skills you will use in this chapter

- ✓ **Being Creative**
- ✓ **Being Literate**
- ✓ **Being Numerate**
- ✓ **Communicating**
- ✓ **Managing Information and Thinking**
- ✓ **Managing Myself**
- ✓ **Staying Well**
- ✓ **Working with Others**

Wellbeing indicator in this chapter

Key words

- Bunreacht na hÉireann
- Articles
- Amended
- Referendum
- Oireachtas
- President
- Áras an Uachtaráin
- Dáil Éireann
- TDs
- Leinster House
- Constituencies
- Independents
- Election campaigns
- Canvassing
- Majority government
- Coalition government
- Taoiseach
- Tánaiste
- Minister
- Cabinet
- Government departments
- Budget
- Attorney General
- Civil service
- Seanad Éireann
- Senators
- Cathaoirleach
- Local government
- Councillors
- Electoral register
- Electorate
- Local elections
- By-elections
- General elections
- Presidential elections
- European elections
- Polling card
- Polling station
- Polling clerk
- Ballot paper
- Polling booth
- Ballot box
- Quota
- Total valid poll
- Spoiled votes
- Eliminated
- Returning Officer
- Proportional representation
- Opposition
- Collective cabinet responsibility
- Minority government

Ireland: A democratic state

Ireland's constitution is called **Bunreacht na hÉireann** and was enacted in 1937 when it was accepted by the Irish people. The constitution is a legal document that describes how Ireland should be governed. It is divided into a series of fifty **articles**. The main articles are set out below.

Bunreacht na hÉireann
Constitution of Ireland

Articles 1–11:	The Irish nation and state
Articles 12–14:	The roles and powers of the Irish President
Articles 15–28:	Describes how the government is organised
Article 29:	Describes international relations between Ireland and the wider world
Articles 30–33:	Describes the role of government advisors such as the Attorney General
Articles 34–39:	Explains the Irish court system
Articles 40–44:	Refers to the rights of Irish citizens, family rights, education rights, the right to own private property and religious rights
Article 45:	Sets out Ireland's social policy – this is the way in which the state looks after the welfare of its citizens
Articles 46–50:	Describes how the constitution can be **amended**, or rewritten

Society is in a constant state of change. Laws reflect these changes and sometimes help change. The constitution may need to be amended or changed when laws change. Since Ireland is a democracy and the power is in the hands of the people, the constitution cannot be changed unless the majority of people in Ireland agree to do so. To change the constitution, the government must hold a **referendum**.

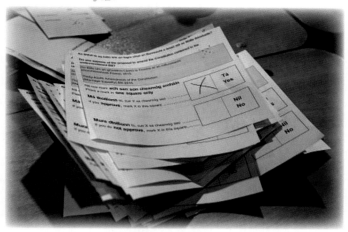

In 2015 the Irish people were asked to vote on the marriage equality referendum

How Ireland is governed

Ireland's national parliament is called the **Oireachtas**. The main role of the Oireachtas is to govern the country and make laws on behalf of the citizens. The Oireachtas is made up of the President and the two houses of the Oireachtas:

🌐 Dáil Éireann (House of Representatives)

🌐 Seanad Éireann (Senate).

The Irish President (Uachtarán na hÉireann)

The Irish **President** is the head of state in Ireland. The President is elected by the Irish people for a term of seven years. The President can serve no more than two terms in office. The official residence of the President is **Áras an Uachtaráin** in Dublin's Phoenix Park.

Bunreacht na hÉireann outlines the role and powers of the President. These include:

🌐 Safeguarding the constitution

🌐 Signing bills so that they become law

🌐 Ensuring that proposed laws don't infringe on the rights of Irish citizens

🌐 Representing Ireland abroad

🌐 Acting as commander-in-chief of the Irish defence forces

🌐 Giving new government ministers their seal of office.

Irish presidential roll of honour

Douglas Hyde – elected 1938

Seán T. Ó Ceallaigh – elected 1945

Éamon de Valera – elected 1959

Erskine Childers – elected 1973

Cearbhall Ó Dálaigh – elected 1974

Patrick Hillery – elected 1976

Mary Robinson – elected 1990

Mary McAleese – elected 1997

Michael D. Higgins – elected 2011

Dáil Éireann

Dáil Éireann is the name given to Ireland's national parliament. The Dáil is made up of 160 **TDs (Teachtaí Dála)**. The Dáil sits at **Leinster House** in Dublin.

Leinster House, Dublin

Ireland is divided into 39 areas called **constituencies**. The people in each constituency can elect three, four or five TDs to the Dáil. The number of TDs each constituency elects depends on the size of the population in that area.

TDs play an important role in the Dáil. They represent the interests of the people living in their constituencies. They debate local and national issues. They can propose and pass new laws. TDs are also members of committees that investigate issues or review proposed laws.

TDs don't spend all of their time in the Dáil. It is important that they also meet with the people in their constituency. To do this, TDs hold clinics where they can listen to constituents and advise them on a wide range of issues.

Most TDs belong to a political party. Some TDs run as **independents**. Every candidate and party has its own vision as to how the country should be run. The main political parties are:

Video Smartvote.ie

During elections, political parties try to influence people to vote for candidates representing their party. Parties run **election campaigns** to encourage people to vote. Candidates use posters, social media platforms and advertising to encourage people to vote for them or for their party.

Many candidates like to meet voters personally, so they call to their houses during election time to speak to them. This is called **canvassing**.

Imagine!

- ✓ Being Creative
- ✓ Being Literate
- ✓ Communicating
- ✓ Managing Information and Thinking
- ✓ Managing Myself

Imagine that you have formed a new political party.

- ❯ What is the name of your political party?
- ❯ Draw the logo for your new political party.
- ❯ What three issues would you like your political party to highlight?
- ❯ Draw a poster to encourage people to vote for you.

The government

The government is decided by a **general election**. The political party or parties that win the most seats in the election form the government. There are different forms of governments in Ireland.

A **majority government** is formed by the political party that wins the majority of seats in a general election. To get a majority, a political party has to win at least 50% plus one seat in the general election.

If no party has won a majority of seats, two or more political parties or independent TDs can come together to form the government. This is called a **coalition government**.

Sometimes a political party or coalition does not have a majority of seats in the Dáil. In this case they can form a **minority government**.

Do you know what type of government we currently have?

Political parties and independent TDs who are not in government are called the **opposition**. The role of the opposition is to question government policy and government decisions. The opposition are important, since they make the government accountable for its actions and decisions. Having a strong opposition is a hallmark of a healthy democracy.

The role of the government

The government is responsible for running the affairs of the Irish state and making decisions on behalf of its citizens. The main roles of the government include:

- Making new laws
- Managing the finances of the country
- Managing the economy
- Looking after the social affairs of the people
- Providing and improving key services
- Forging links and working in partnership with other countries
- Working in partnership with the EU
- Planning for the future.

The Taoiseach

The **Taoiseach** is the head of government and is usually the leader of the largest political party in the Dáil. The Taoiseach must provide leadership and also control government business.

The Taoiseach acts as a spokesperson for the government and defends government decisions. The Taoiseach also plays an important role in developing the relationship between Ireland and our EU partners and other countries.

The Taoiseach appoints a **Tánaiste**, who acts as deputy Taoiseach and head of government when the Taoiseach is absent.

The government has many responsibilities, and it would be impossible for the Taoiseach to handle them alone. Therefore, the Taoiseach assembles a team of people to help them carry out the work of the government. The Taoiseach appoints **ministers** who are in charge of a particular government department.

The cabinet

The **cabinet** is the main decision-making body of the government. The cabinet consists of the Taoiseach, the Tánaiste and the ministers in charge of each of the government departments. The cabinet meets on a regular basis to make decisions on key issues affecting Ireland. Once decisions are made, members of the cabinet must publicly support the decisions made. This is called **collective cabinet responsibility**.

The **Attorney General** also attends cabinet meetings. Although they are not a member of the government, the Attorney General acts as chief legal adviser to the government. The Attorney General has to ensure that any government decisions are legal and constitutional. The Attorney General is often consulted when the government is preparing new laws.

Government departments

Government departments look after the social, economic, political and cultural affairs of the state. The Taoiseach appoints ministers to take charge of each department. Each minister must ensure the smooth running of their department. They may also have to make important decisions about issues relevant to their government department.

Department of Finance

This department is responsible for the financial affairs of the country. The Minister for Finance makes important decisions about the finances of the state. He or she decides how much money needs

to be raised in taxes and how much money each government department is given. This department also controls government spending. Every year, the Minister for Finance draws up a budget that sets out how much money the government needs to take in and how much it needs to spend.

Who is the current Minister for Finance?

Department of Health

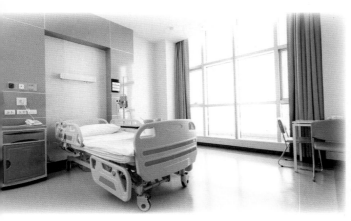

This department is responsible for the health and wellbeing of people living in Ireland. It provides health services and is responsible for our hospitals and for recruiting and paying the salaries of healthcare staff such as doctors and nurses. This department also promotes healthy living and is responsible for campaigns that encourage citizens to lead healthy lives. The Minister for Health is responsible for managing this department. The Minister for Health played a key role during the Covid-19 pandemic and was involved in making decisions to ensure the health and safety of Irish people.

Who is the current Minister for Health?

Department of Social Protection

This department is responsible for promoting active participation and inclusion in society. The Minister for Social Protection is responsible for this department. This department provides income supports and employment services to people who need them. Income supports include Jobseeker's Benefit, Illness Benefit, the State Pension and Child Benefit. This department also provides employment support services and training to people seeking employment.

An Roinn Coimirce Sóisialaí
Department of Social Protection
www.welfare.ie

Who is the current Minister for Social Protection?

The civil service

The **civil service** is the administrative arm of the government. Its main role is to advise the government on policy and carry out the day-to-day running of government departments. Members of the civil service have a duty to carry out decisions made by the government.

Seanad Éireann

Seanad Éireann consists of sixty members, called **senators**. Senators are either elected to the Seanad or nominated by the Taoiseach. The sixty members are organised as follows:

🌐 Forty-three senators are elected to the Seanad by TDs and city and county councillors. These senators are elected from five panels that represent important areas in Irish society.

🌐 Six senators are elected by university graduates of the National University of Ireland and the University of Dublin (Trinity College). Only university graduates from these universities can vote in the Seanad elections.

🌐 The remaining eleven senators are nominated by the Taoiseach.

The five Seanad panels are:

1 Culture and Education

2 Agriculture

3 Labour

4 Industry and Commerce

5 Public Administration

The Seanad chamber inside Leinster House

The Seanad is less powerful than the Dáil, but it does play an important role.

🌐 Members of the Seanad debate important issues. Members examine any new bills sent from the Dáil. This ensures that laws are not enacted too quickly.

🌐 The Seanad can also propose new laws.

🌐 Seanad Éireann business is presided over by a chairperson called the **Cathaoirleach**.

Debate

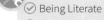
- ✓ Being Literate
- ✓ Communicating
- ✓ Managing Information and Thinking
- ✓ Managing Myself
- ✓ Working with Others

Many argue that Seanad elections are not inclusive because only TDs, councillors, some university graduates and the Taoiseach can elect or nominate senators. Organise a debate on the following topic:

💬 'Seanad elections are not democratic.'
Having completed this debate, has your opinion changed or remained the same? Can you explain why?

Local government

Every household in Ireland is served by a local government. These local governments are called local authorities. The main role of local authorities is to provide vital services to householders in local areas. They are also responsible for providing and maintaining local amenities such as parks, pitches, leisure centres, libraries and civic spaces.

There are three different forms of local authority in Ireland:

1 County councils

2 City councils

3 City and county councils

Services provided by local authorities include:

🌐 Housing, accommodation and building

🌐 Road transport and safety

🌐 Water supply and sewage

🌐 Recreation and local amenities

🌐 Development incentives and controls

🌐 Environmental protection.

Who is the local authority?

Local authorities are democratic because the people living within in each local authority area elect the representatives to represent their interests at local level. These representatives are called **councillors** and are elected every five years through local elections. Councillors attend monthly meetings and make important decisions about their local authority areas. Each councillor is entitled to vote on issues proposed at council meetings. These issues include the annual council budget and how this money is spent, housing policy and environmental protection policies.

Most local authorities have a Chief Executive Officer (CEO). The CEO is responsible for the day-to-day running of the local authority. He or she is also responsible for making key decisions related to planning permission, allocating local authority housing and local authority staffing.

Representatives and councillors often attend public meetings to discuss issues that affect the local area.

Local authorities work closely with people living within their community. Local people are often consulted when the local authority wants to make changes to the local environment. Representatives from local government can attend public meetings or meetings with residence associations to discuss proposed changes or developments in the local area. Local people are often invited to take part in questionnaires and surveys to give their thoughts and opinions to changes such as traffic restrictions or the development of a new amenity. This ensures that local people play a part in the decision-making process.

Elections

Elections are often considered to be the backbone of democracy. This is because citizens have the power to vote for representatives who act on their behalf. Irish citizens living in Ireland can vote in elections when they reach eighteen years of age and their name appears on the electoral register. The **electoral register** is a list of all the people eligible to vote in an election. People eligible to vote are called the **electorate**. Irish citizens are entitled to vote in the following elections:

- 🌐 **Local elections:** Local elections are held every five years to elect councillors to local authorities.

- 🌐 **By-elections:** These elections take place when a Dáil seat becomes vacant. This can happen when a TD resigns or if he or she dies while in office.

- 🌐 **General elections:** A general election occurs every five years or when the Dáil is dissolved.

- 🌐 **Presidential elections:** These elections occur every seven years.

- 🌐 **European elections:** European elections take place every five years. MEPs to the European Parliament are elected.

The voting process

Prior to an election or a referendum, all those eligible to vote receive a **polling card** in the post. The polling card has the voter's name and address and the location of the local **polling station**. The polling station is usually located in a primary school or community hall.

On the day of an election, you hand your polling card to the **polling clerk**, who marks your name off a list. This helps to calculate the turnout at the election, as well as ensuring that nobody votes more than once.

You are then given a **ballot paper** with the names, in alphabetical order, of all the election candidates. The ballot paper also states whether or not the candidate is connected to a political party.

Elections in Ireland are held by secret ballot. Therefore, **polling booths** are provided in polling stations so that you can vote in private. Voters indicate their preference by writing 1 beside the candidate they want to represent them, 2 beside their second preference, and so on.

When you have cast your vote, you place your ballot paper in a **ballot box**. When the polling station closes, the ballot box is brought to a count centre, where the votes are counted.

Counting the votes

When ballot boxes reach the count centre, they are emptied onto a table. Before the count begins, a **quota** is calculated. This is the number of votes a candidate needs to be elected. For example:

$$\text{Quota} = \frac{\text{Total valid poll}}{\text{Number of seats} + 1} + 1$$

The **total valid poll** is calculated by counting the number of votes cast and subtracting the number of **spoiled votes**. A spoiled vote is a ballot paper that has been filled out incorrectly or has been defaced in some way.

Being Numerate

Total number of votes cast	**45,000**
Spoiled votes	**− 450**
Total valid poll	**44,550**
To calculate the quota:	
Total valid poll	**44,550**
Divided by numer of seats + 1	**5**
=	**8,910**
+	**1**
Quota:	**8,911**

In the example above, 8,911 is the quota. This means that the candidates need 8,911 votes to be elected.

Once the quota has been established, the count begins. The first count sorts out how many number 1 votes each candidate has. If someone reaches the quota, they are elected. If they have votes to spare, their votes are transferred to the second choices on the ballot paper.

If no one reaches the quota after the first count, the candidate with the least votes is **eliminated**. Their votes are transferred, so their votes go to the second choices on the ballot paper.

This process is repeated until all the seats in an election have been filled. The result of the election is announced by the **Returning Officer**.

The system of voting in Ireland is called **proportional representation (PR)**. This means the number of seats a political party wins is in proportion to the number of votes it gets. In other words, if a party gets 10% of the votes, it should get 10% of the seats.

Take action!

Being Literate
Communicating
Working with Others

Organise a visit to Leinster House to see Dáil Éireann and Seanad Éireann in action. Visits can be organised through your local TD.

Don't forget to complete your reflections in your reflective journal.

European democratic institutions

Learning outcomes

By the end of this chapter you should know the key democratic institutions and structures in Europe. You should be able to explain the roles and workings of the Council of Europe and the European Parliament.

Key words

- European citizenship
- Council of Europe
- Committee of Ministers
- Parliamentary Assembly
- Congress of Local and Regional Authorities
- Secretariat
- European Court of Human Rights
- European Union
- European Commission
- Commissioners
- European Parliament
- Members of the European Parliament (MEPs)
- Council of the European Union
- Council of Ministers
- Court of Auditors
- European Central Bank

Key skills you will use in this chapter

- ✓ Being Creative
- ✓ Being Literate
- ✓ Being Numerate
- ✓ Communicating
- ✓ Managing Information and Thinking
- ✓ Managing Myself
- ✓ Staying Well
- ✓ Working with Others

Wellbeing indicator in this chapter

European citizenship

In Strand 1, you learned that you are a member of many communities. One such community is the European community. Evidence of your **European citizenship** is not hard to find.

Your passport states that you are not only an Irish citizen, but also a citizen of the European Union

You use the euro currency

Since the end of the Second World War, European countries have made greater efforts to co-operate and work together to protect the rights of their citizens and to help European states progress economically. Two democratic institutions emerged after the Second World War to bring about these goals:

1   The Council of Europe

2   The European Union.

Many of the roads and bridges you travel on were funded by the European Union, such as this one in Scotland

The Council of Europe

The **Council of Europe** was set up in 1949, after the end of the Second World War, to create a lasting peace and to improve the lives of European citizens. The main aims of this organisation are the promotion and protection of human rights, promoting democracy and protecting the rule of law.

COUNCIL OF EUROPE

CONSEIL DE L'EUROPE

In 2018, there were 47 member states representing over 800 million European citizens. Ireland has been a member of the Council of Europe since it was set up in 1949. The Council of Europe sits at Strasbourg in France.

Council of Europe   Conseil de l'Europe

The Council of Europe is a completely separate organisation from the European Union (EU), even though it works very closely with it

Research

Find out which member states of the Council of Europe are not members of the EU.

- ⊘ Being Literate
- ⊘ Managing Information and Thinking
- ⊘ Managing Myself

Structure of the Council of Europe

The Committee of Ministers

The **Committee of Ministers** is the decision-making arm of the Council of Europe. It meets twice a year and is made up of the foreign ministers from each of the member states. However, some are permanent members who meet once a month.

The Parliamentary Assembly

The main role of the **Parliamentary Assembly** is to debate issues common to all member states. The assembly is made up of members who are appointed by the national parliaments of each member state. Ireland currently has four representatives in the assembly.

The Congress of Local and Regional Authorities

The aim of the **Congress of Local and Regional Authorities** is to develop co-operation between member states. It also promotes co-operation between regions within members states. For example, it helps to develop cross-border co-operation between the Republic of Ireland and Northern Ireland.

The Secretariat

The **secretariat** carries out the day-to-day work of the Council of Europe. The Council consists of almost 2,000 people who work in Strasbourg.

Achievements of the Council of Europe

🌐 In 1950, the Council of Europe drafted the European Convention on Human Rights. This sets out the rights and freedoms of European citizens.

The European Court of Human Rights was set up by the Council of Europe in 1959

🌐 **The European Court of Human Rights** sits in Strasbourg. One judge from each of the member states works in this court. The main function of this court is to rule on allegations of human rights violations. European citizens can bring their case to this court if they feel their rights have been violated by a member state.

🌐 The Council of Europe has a proven track record in defending human rights. It helped to abolish the death penalty in member states, it takes cases against racism, discrimination and homophobia and it promotes gender equality.

🌐 In 1955, the Council of Europe adopted the European flag. It has a blue background and 12 yellow stars arranged in a circle.

The stars represent unity between member states. This flag is also used by the European Union.

Research

⊘ Being Literate
⊘ Communicating
⊘ Managing Information and Thinking
⊘ Managing Myself

Find out more about the work of the Council of Europe by visiting its website.

The European Union (EU)

The **European Union** is a group of countries that work together to improve the way people live and how business is conducted in Europe. Member states pay money every year to be a member. The EU uses this money to help to develop member states and to improve the lives of European citizens.

The EU has three main aims:

1 Promoting social and economic progress.

2 Promoting European citizenship and protecting the rights of EU citizens, such as:

🌐 The freedom to move between countries. This enables citizens to live and work in any member state.

🌐 The right to vote in European elections.

3 Developing EU law that protects the rights of citizens.

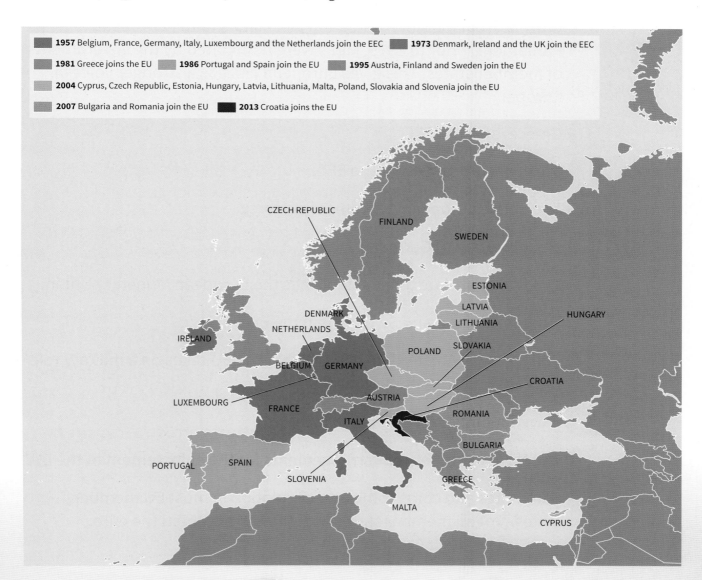

- 1957 Belgium, France, Germany, Italy, Luxembourg and the Netherlands join the EEC
- 1973 Denmark, Ireland and the UK join the EEC
- 1981 Greece joins the EU
- 1986 Portugal and Spain join the EU
- 1995 Austria, Finland and Sweden join the EU
- 2004 Cyprus, Czech Republic, Estonia, Hungary, Latvia, Lithuania, Malta, Poland, Slovakia and Slovenia join the EU
- 2007 Bulgaria and Romania join the EU
- 2013 Croatia joins the EU

The EU has been shaped by many events over the years

1950 Robert Schuman, a French foreign minister, proposes that European countries should pool their iron and steel resources. This led to the formation of the European Coal and Steel Community.

1957 The Treaty of Rome establishes the European Economic Community (EEC) with six members. The founding member states were Belgium, the Federal Republic of Germany, France, Italy, Luxembourg and the Netherlands. The EEC was later (1993) incorporated into the European Union (EU).

1973 Denmark, Ireland and the United Kingdom join the EEC.

1979 The first direct elections to the European Parliament take place. Citizens from member states can elect MEPs to the European Parliament. Prior to 1979, MEPs were nominated by the governments of member states. This gives European citizens a stronger voice in Europe.

1981 Greece joins the EEC.

1986 Spain and Portugal join the EEC.

1987 The Single European Act comes into force.

1990 Reunification of Germany.

1992 The Treaty of Maastricht establishes the European Monetary Union.

1995 Austria, Finland and Sweden join the EU.

1997 The Treaty of Amsterdam ensures that the EU takes on a military role in peace enforcement and peacekeeping.

1999 Eleven member states launch the euro.

2000 The Nice Treaty sets out arrangements for the enlargement of the EU.

2002 Euro notes and coins come into circulation in most EU member states. Not all member states (e.g. the UK) accepted the euro.

2004 Ten new states join the EU during Ireland's presidency: Cyprus, Czech Republic, Estonia, Hungary, Latvia, Lithuania, Malta, Poland, Slovakia and Slovenia.

2007 Bulgaria and Romania join the EU.

2008 Ireland rejects the Lisbon Treaty.

2009 Ireland ratifies the Lisbon Treaty.

2013 Croatia joins the EU.

2016 The UK holds a referendum to ask if the UK should remain in the EU. Citizens in the UK vote to leave the EU ('Brexit').

2021 The UK leaves the European Union.

Structure of the EU

The EU is composed of five main institutions:

1 The European Commission

2 The European Parliament

3 The Council of the European Union

4 The European Court of Auditors

5 The European Court of Justice (see page 246).

The European Commission

The **European Commission** is made up of **commissioners** from every member state. These commissioners held a political position in their own country. As members of the commission, they are expected to act in the interests of the EU and not take instructions from their own government. The commission is made up of twenty-eight commissioners.

The commission's roles include:

🌐 Developing new laws

🌐 Drawing up the European budget and deciding how this money should be spent

🌐 Enforcing European law

🌐 Representing the European Union internationally.

Video How the European Parliament works

The European Parliament

The **European Parliament** is often called 'the voice of the people'. Since 1979, **members of the European Parliament (MEPs)** have been directly elected by citizens of EU member states. European elections occur every five years. The parliament is based in Belgium, France and Luxembourg.

The European Parliament has three main functions:

1 To legislate – this means it has the power to debate new laws that come from the commission. It votes on whether or not these laws should be passed.

2 The parliament supervises all EU institutions to ensure that they are carrying out their responsibilities.

3 The parliament also has authority over the EU budget and it monitors EU spending.

Currently 11 MEPs represent Ireland in the European Parliament. These MEPs are democratically elected by Irish citizens in European elections.

The Council of the European Union

The **Council of the European Union** is made up of the heads of state of EU member states. As well as the European Parliament, this institution can also decide on new EU laws. The council has a presidency that changes every six months. The council meets twice a year and each meeting takes place in the country that holds the presidency. The country that holds the presidency also decides on the issues that need to be discussed at these meetings.

The Council of Ministers

The **Council of Ministers** is made up of one minister from each EU member state. What minister attends these meetings depends on the issues being discussed. If the issue is agriculture, then the ministers for agriculture from each of the member states would gather. This meeting would be known as the Agricultural Council.

There are other institutions in the EU:

- 🌐 The **Court of Auditors** looks after the EU's financial affairs, ensures that all EU taxes are collected and supervises the EU budget.
- 🌐 The **European Central Bank** seeks to safeguard the value of the euro and to maintain price stability in Eurozone countries.

Benefits of EU membership

Ireland joined the EEC (EU from 1993) in 1973. Membership has had many benefits for Ireland, including the following:

- 🌐 Irish workers can move freely and work without any restrictions in the EU.
- 🌐 EU money has provided jobs, education and training for Irish citizens.
- 🌐 Ireland's roads, railways, ports and airports have been improved thanks to money from the EU.
- 🌐 Irish agriculture has received billions of euro in subsidies from the EU.
- 🌐 Irish fishing ports have improved due to EU Structural Funds.
- 🌐 Ireland benefits from people and industries from other member states who invest in its economy.

 **Take action!**

- ✓ Being Creative
- ✓ Being Literate
- ✓ Communicating
- ✓ Managing Information and Thinking
- ✓ Managing Myself
- ✓ Working with Others

Europe Day is celebrated on 9 May each year.
Organise a celebration of Europe Day in your school.

 Don't forget to complete your reflections in your reflective journal.

The strengths and weaknesses of the democratic process

Learning outcomes

By the end of this chapter you should be able to put forward arguments showing both the strengths and weaknesses of the democratic process.

Key skills you will use in this chapter

- ✓ Being Creative
- ✓ Being Literate
- ✓ Being Numerate
- ✓ Communicating
- ✓ Managing Information and Thinking
- ✓ Managing Myself
- ✓ Staying Well
- ✓ Working with Others

Key words

- 🔑 Corruption
- 🔑 Turnout
- 🔑 Gender quotas

Wellbeing indicators in this chapter

Strengths of the democratic process

① People's interests are protected

By having a right to vote, people have a role in making major decisions that affect their country.

② It prevents one person or group from claiming control

In democratic states, elected representatives have a set amount of time in power. When this time is up, they must put themselves up for re-election if they want to remain in power. Look at the graph on presidential term limits in European republics in your reflective journal and complete the questions there.

Create a video

Divide into groups. In your group, create a short video explaining the strengths of the democratic process.

- ✓ Being Creative
- ✓ Being Literate
- ✓ Communicating
- ✓ Managing Information and Thinking
- ✓ Managing Myself
- ✓ Working with Others

Weaknesses of the democratic process

① It may lead to corruption

Corruption means illegal, bad or dishonest behaviour, especially by people in power. Some politicians use their positions of power for personal gain. This goes against the principles of democracy. Elected representatives should serve the people and not use their positions to benefit personally.

Unfortunately, we have had experience of corruption in Ireland. One example is planning corruption. In the past, some politicians received money from developers in exchange for changing planning laws to suit the developers.

② Voting is not mandatory

The right to vote is central to the democratic process. In Ireland, as in most democracies, it is not a legal requirement for citizens to vote. A small number of democracies, including Australia, enforce mandatory voting. Some argue that this undermines democracy, while others say the opposite. In the Irish general election of 2016, large numbers of people who were entitled to vote did not vote. The number or percentage of people who vote is called the **turnout**.

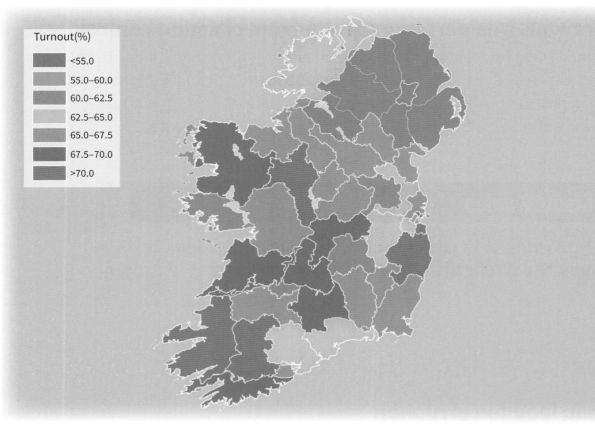

Turnout(%)

	<55.0
	55.0–60.0
	60.0–62.5
	62.5–65.0
	65.0–67.5
	67.5–70.0
	>70.0

Map of voter turnout, based on analysis by Dr Adrian Kavanagh, Department of Geography, Maynooth University, March 2016

Questions

- ⊘ Being Literate
- ⊘ Being Numerate
- ⊘ Managing Information and Thinking
- ⊘ Managing Myself

Examine the map above, which shows voter turnout for each Dáil constituency in the 2016 general election.

1 In your copybook, name three constituencies with a turnout greater than 70%.

2 What was the turnout in your constituency?

3 Where was the lowest turnout in the country? Why, do you think, was the turnout so low there?

③ It can take a long time to make decisions

In a democracy, to give people the right to be properly represented, many steps need to be taken before decisions are made. For example, it takes five separate stages for laws to be passed in Ireland.

4 Democracies often don't represent women

Women are not fairly represented in political positions in many democratic societies. While we have had two female Presidents, the number of female representatives in Dáil Éireann is low. In order to increase the number of female representatives, a bill was passed into law in 2012 that said female candidates

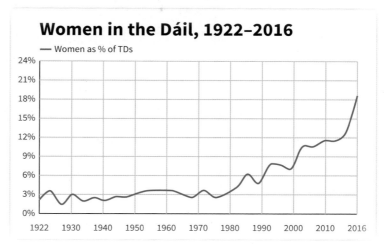

Women in the Dáil, 1922–2016

— Women as % of TDs

Source: Journal.ie

must account for 30% of the total number of electoral candidates in the 2016 general election, with a view to increasing this to 40% by 2023. We refer to this as the introduction of **gender quotas**. This is an attempt to reflect the fact that the country is 50% female and 50% male.

Debate

Organise a walking debate on the following topic:

> 'Is the introduction of gender quotas a disadvantage to anyone?'

Having completed the debate, has your opinion changed or remained the same? Can you explain why?

- ✓ Being Creative
- ✓ Being Literate
- ✓ Communicating
- ✓ Managing Information and Thinking
- ✓ Managing Myself
- ✓ Working with Others

Take action!

Organise a mock referendum for your year group. The referendum should be based on the proposal to change the constitution in order to make voting mandatory in Ireland.

- ✓ Being Literate
- ✓ Being Numerate
- ✓ Communicating
- ✓ Managing Information and Thinking
- ✓ Managing Myself
- ✓ Working with Others

Don't forget to complete your reflections in your reflective journal.

How the law directly relates to me

Learning outcomes

By the end of this chapter you will be able to identify some laws that directly relate to your life. You will also be able to explain how the law relates to people around you.

Key skills you will use in this chapter

- ✓ **Being Creative**
- ✓ **Being Literate**
- ✓ **Being Numerate**
- ✓ **Communicating**
- ✓ **Managing Information and Thinking**
- ✓ **Managing Myself**
- ✓ **Staying Well**
- ✓ **Working with Others**

Key words

- ⚷ Rules
- ⚷ Laws
- ⚷ Consumer
- ⚷ Consumer law
- ⚷ Sale of Goods and Supply of Services Act
- ⚷ Illegal
- ⚷ Competition and Consumer Protection Commission
- ⚷ Office of the Ombudsman

Wellbeing indicators in this chapter

Rules

Being a secondary school student, you will have probably noticed how school **rules** impact on your daily life in school. Although you may not agree with some of the rules, it is important to understand why we have rules.

School rules exist so that students can learn in a safe, healthy and peaceful environment. These rules aim to promote wellbeing within the school community. Most organisations, such as sports clubs, youth clubs and places of work, have rules.

No running

QUIET PLEASE

Imagine!

Your school has decided to have a 'No School Rules Day'. Write a diary entry in your copybook describing what life was like for students and teachers on that day.

- ⊘ Being Creative
- ⊘ Being Literate
- ⊘ Communicating
- ⊘ Managing Myself

Laws

Laws are rules or regulations. Laws are important to the community and society because they give guidance with regard to conduct and order. Laws safeguard the rights of citizens. They also inform individuals about their responsibilities towards others, their communities and the environment.

From the time you got up this morning, your life has been influenced by laws.

🌐 You may have had cereal for your breakfast this morning. The law states that the ingredients and nutritional information must be displayed on the packaging of any foodstuffs.

Nutrition Facts
Serving Size 3/4 cup

Amount Per Serving	
Calories 110 Calories from Fat 15	
	% Daily Value*
Total Fat 1.5g	**2%**
Saturated Fat 0g	
Trans Fat 0g	
Cholesterol 0mg	**0%**
Sodium 160mg	**7%**
Total Carbohydrate 22g	**7%**
Dietary Fiber 2g	**8%**
Sugars 9g	
Protein 2g	

Vitamin A 10%	Vitamin C 10%
Calcium 10%	Iron 25%

*Percentage Daily Values based on 2,000 calorie diet.

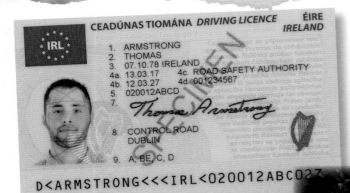

Maybe you took a bus to school. The law states that the driver of the bus must have a valid driving licence and have the vehicle taxed and insured. The law also states that the driver must drive responsibly and obey traffic laws.

Your right to an education is also protected by the law. The law ensures that every child has the right to an education.

Can you think of some other laws that influence your daily life?

Think, pair and share

- ✓ Being Creative
- ✓ Being Literate
- ✓ Communicating
- ✓ Managing Information and Thinking
- ✓ Managing Myself
- ✓ Working with Others

The law affects people in different ways. Look at the people in the photographs below and at the top of the page opposite.

Think about laws that influence their lives. For each person, write down one law that affects them. Now turn to your partner and listen to their thoughts. Are they similar to or different from your own ideas? With your partner, decide what information you would like to share with the class group. Use the table in your reflective journal to write down your ideas.

1   A publican

2   A landlord

| 3 | A dog owner | 4 | A secondary school student | 5 | A builder |

Imagine!

Imagine that a ship you have been travelling on has become stranded on a deserted island.

There are twenty other passengers stranded with you. You have radio contact but you have been informed that due to stormy conditions, help will not reach you for two weeks. There is enough food and water for everyone for eight days.

- Being Creative
- Being Literate
- Communicating
- Managing Information and Thinking
- Managing Myself

The group has elected you as the leader. As leader, name five laws you would make to ensure the health and safety of everyone on the island. For each law, give a reason why you made it.

Young people and the law

Your life is affected by various laws. Starting when you are a baby, your parents must, by law, register your birth.

Education

🌐 A child must start school before they reach the age of six.

🌐 You may not leave school until you are at least sixteen years old.

▶ **Video** Work rights for under-18s

Employment

⊕ A fourteen-year-old is not permitted to work during the school term. She or he can work up to thirty-five hours per week during school holidays.

⊕ A fifteen-year-old can work up to eight hours per week during the school term and no more than thirty-five hours per week during school holidays.

Driving a vehicle

⊕ You must be at least sixteen to drive a moped up to 45 kph.

⊕ You must be at least seventeen years old to drive a car.

Criminal law

⊕ The age of criminal responsibility in Ireland is twelve years old. This means that children under the age of twelve cannot be charged with an offence.

⊕ However, in the case of serious offences, such as murder and manslaughter, a ten- or an eleven-year-old can be charged.

Consumer law

One area of law that affects most citizens is consumer law.

Every day, people buy goods in shops, supermarkets and online. A **consumer** is the name given to any person who buys goods or services.

Consumers are entitled to rights and these are protected under **consumer law**. Consumer law outlines the rights and responsibilities of consumers and of those who sell goods and services. One of the most important laws in this area is the **Sale of Goods and Supply of Services Act, 1980**.

Under this law, goods purchased by the consumer must:

1 Be of merchantable and reasonable quality

2 Be fit for the purpose intended

3 Match their description and be as described in advertising or labelling

4 Be the same as the sample shown

If you are unhappy with the quality of an item you have purchased, you may be entitled to a replacement, a refund or a repair.

This Act also protects consumers who buy or avail of services. Under the Sale of Goods and Supply of Services Act, 1980:

1 **The person providing the service must be qualified or have the skill to provide that service.**

2 **The service must be provided with care and diligence.**

3 **The service must be of a high standard and quality.**

Consumer law also ensures that the use of particular signs in shops is **illegal**, such as the sign below.

NO REFUND

Questions

- ✓ Being Literate
- ✓ Managing Information and Thinking
- ✓ Managing Myself

Read the following scenarios and decide whether they are covered by consumer law. Give a reason why each situation is or is not covered by consumer law.

1 Ailbhe contracted a builder to build a small porch. When it was completed, Ailbhe noticed that the bricks were uneven. She later learned that the bricklayer was an apprentice still learning his trade.

2 Matilda bought a new jacket in a shop. When she got home, she decided that she didn't like it.

3 Jan bought a state-of-the-art washing machine for his new house, costing him €700. Two months later, the washing machine broke down.

Competition and Consumer Protection Commission

The **Competition and Consumer Protection Commission (CCPC)** was set up to enforce consumer protection laws, look after the interests of consumers and raise awareness about consumer rights in Ireland. This commission has a consumer helpline and website to help consumers to get more information on their consumer rights.

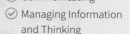

Coimisiún um
Iomaíocht agus
Cosaint Tomhaltóirí

Competition and
Consumer Protection
Commission

Research

- ✓ Being Literate
- ✓ Communicating
- ✓ Managing Information and Thinking
- ✓ Managing Myself

To find out more about the work of the CCPC and your consumer rights, log on to the CCPC website.

European Consumer Centre

Online shopping has become popular during the past decade. You can buy goods using the internet and a bank card. However, the popularity of online shopping has given rise to online scamming. People think that they are buying a particular make of a product but unwittingly buy fake goods.

The European Consumer Centre (ECC) is part-funded by the CCPC and European Commission and is part of an EU-wide network. The ECC provides free advice and assistance to consumers who have disputes with traders based in another EU country. They produced the infographic on the next page to help consumers to avoid buying fake products on the internet.

Cabhair agus comhairle do thomhaltóirí san Eoraip ECC-Net

European Consumer Centre Ireland

Help and advice for consumers in Europe — ECC-Net — Co-funded by the European Union

10 ECC-Net tips on how you can avoid buying fake products on the Internet.

Check the identity of the seller

Search other consumers' reviews

Check whether the website benefits from a trust mark

Assess the general layout of the website

Check your consumer rights on the trader's website

Check the picture of the product

Watch the price of the good

authorised
black-listed

Check the official website for authorised sellers

https://

Pay with a secured means of payment

(Nearly) new

Pay attention to refurbished products

The Office of the Ombudsman

Every day, people avail of services provided by public bodies (such as An Post and the HSE), local authorities or government departments. If somebody feels that they have been treated unfairly by any of these bodies, they are entitled to make a complaint to the **Office of the Ombudsman**. This office investigates complaints in a fair and impartial way.

Ombudsman

Take action!

- ✓ Being Creative
- ✓ Being Literate
- ✓ Communicating
- ✓ Managing Information and Thinking
- ✓ Managing Myself
- ✓ Staying Well
- ✓ Working with Others

Produce a booklet for students in your school that outlines their rights as consumers. Your booklet should contain the main points of the Sale of Goods and Supply of Services Act, 1980. It should also include useful consumer tips when buying goods and services in shops or online.

Don't forget to complete your reflections in your reflective journal.

Making and enforcing laws

Learning outcomes

By the end of this chapter you will understand how laws are made, enforced and evolve over time.

Key skills you will use in this chapter

- ✓ Being Creative
- ✓ Being Literate
- ✓ Being Numerate
- ✓ Communicating
- ✓ Managing Information and Thinking
- ✓ Managing Myself
- ✓ Staying Well
- ✓ Working with Others

Wellbeing indicators in this chapter

Key words

- Brehon law
- Brehons
- Common law
- Irish Free State
- Bill
- Committee stage
- Report stage
- Constitutional
- Act
- Judiciary
- Case law
- By-laws
- United Nations
- International Law Commission
- Crimes against peace
- War crimes
- Crimes against humanity
- Genocide
- Ethnic cleansing
- An Garda Síochána
- Garda Commissioner
- Minister for Justice and Equality
- Community Garda
- Neighbourhood Watch
- Community Alert

A brief history of Irish law

The legal system in Ireland has developed over hundreds of years and has been shaped by different people and events.

Brehon law was the earliest system of law in Ireland and dates from Celtic times. Brehon law was first written down in the seventh century. Brehon law dealt with civil matters and criminal matters.

Men and women called **Brehons** would travel to villages and towns to sort out disputes and disagreements. Brehon law made sure that the rights of the people were protected and that everyone was treated equally and justly. Those found to have broken Brehon law usually paid a fine or compensation to the injured party.

Some examples of Brehon laws include:

- If a woman is pregnant and craves food and her husband withholds that food, he must pay a fine.

- When you are old, your family must provide you with one oatcake a day and a container of sour milk. Your family must bathe you every twentieth day and wash your head every Saturday.

Irish women had greater freedom, independence and rights to property under Brehon law than women in other European societies of the time. Men and women held their property separately and women and men could leave a marriage on a number of grounds. Research some more Brehon laws – you may be surprised by what you discover!

From the seventeenth century, a number of events changed the law in Ireland. Oliver Cromwell's invasion of Ireland and the victory of William of Orange over King James II meant that Britain could exert more power over Ireland. One way in which it could exert power was by imposing English **common law** on the people of Ireland. The Irish legal system today was based on common law.

Oliver Cromwell

In 1922 the **Irish Free State** was established. The Free State kept much of the common law system and set up its own court system. A constitution was written that was later replaced by Bunreacht na hÉireann in 1937. This set out the law of the land and how Ireland should be governed.

Who makes the law today?

The Oireachtas

Most laws today are made by the Oireachtas (the legislature). Once a new law is proposed, it has to go through a number of stages before it is passed.

Stage 1

When a new law is proposed, it is called a **bill**. A bill can originate (start) either in Dáil Éireann or, in some cases, in Seanad Éireann. A copy of the bill is distributed to all the TDs in Dáil Éireann so that it can be analysed.

Stage 2

Once all TDs have been given an opportunity to analyse the bill, it is then open to debate. After discussion and debate in the Dáil, TDs can suggest changes or amendments to the bill.

Stage 3

This stage is often called the **committee stage**. A special committee of TDs is formed that examines the bill very closely and discusses changes to it.

Stage 4

The bill is rewritten to include any changes. This is called the **report stage** and is the final draft of the bill. No more changes can be made after this stage.

Stage 5

The final draft of the bill goes back to the Dáil. Every TD votes to accept or reject the bill. If it is passed, it is sent to Seanad Éireann for further debate. Senators vote on whether to accept or reject the bill. The bill must be passed by both the Dáil and the Seanad.

Stage 6

If passed by both houses, the bill is sent to the President. The President must decide whether the bill is in line with our constitution. If the President is unsure, she or he may pass the bill to the Supreme Court, which will make a decision as to whether the bill is **constitutional**. If it is found to be constitutional, the bill is signed by the President. Only then can it become law. When the President signs it, the bill becomes an **Act** and is part of Irish law.

The judicary

The **judiciary** is the collective name given to judges. When judges make a judgment on the outcome of a court case, this becomes law. This is called **case law**.

Local authorities

Local authorities can pass local laws called **by-laws**. By-laws are laws that are put in place to look after the needs of a specific area, such as a public park. Common by-laws relate to:

- 🌐 The management and disposal of household and commercial waste
- 🌐 The control of dogs
- 🌐 Parking restrictions, fines and vehicle clamping
- 🌐 Casual trading
- 🌐 Street performance
- 🌐 Drinking alcohol in public places.

The European Union

Ireland joined the European Economic Community in 1973. This later became the European Union. Since joining, Ireland must observe and obey laws made and passed by the European Union.

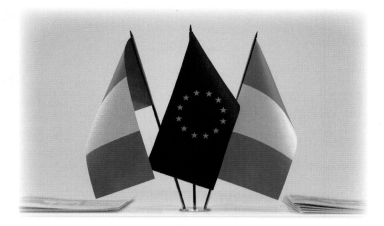

International law

International law is about the relationships between countries. International laws cover areas such as human rights law, criminal law, economic law and environmental law.

International law is made by the **United Nations**, which was founded in 1945. The main aims of the United Nations are to keep peace between countries and to protect human rights worldwide. The United Nations set up a special body called the **International Law Commission** to create and develop international laws. There are thirty-four members of the commission who meet every year to review existing laws and develop new laws. Ireland is a member of the United Nations and is therefore bound by international law.

Under international law, a government can be held accountable for contravening (not obeying) international law. This means that a head of state can be punished if found guilty. The most serious crimes under international law include:

🌐 **Crimes against peace:** This happens when one country starts a war of aggression against another. It can include breaking peace treaties.

🌐 **War crimes:** These crimes include the ill-treatment of prisoners of war, taking hostages and plundering public and private property during war or conflict.

🌐 **Crimes against humanity:** These crimes involve crimes against civilians during a war or a conflict. Such crimes include **genocide** or **ethnic cleansing**.

Enforcing the law in Ireland: The role of An Garda Síochána

An Garda Síochána, or 'Guardians of the Peace', are Ireland's national police service responsible for maintaining law and order. The gardaí do this without carrying guns as weapons.

There are approximately 13,000 gardaí in Ireland. The **Garda Commissioner** is responsible for the control and management of An Garda Síochána. She or he is appointed by the government and must report to the **Minister for Justice and Equality**.

Within An Garda Síochána, there are numerous ranks, with varying levels of responsibility.

The main functions of An Garda Síochána are:

- Traffic management and enforcing road traffic laws
- Responding to calls for assistance in road accidents, violence in the home, burglaries, vandalism and street crime
- Investigating and solving crimes
- Crime prevention.

Members of An Garda Síochána work very closely with communities. Therefore, most Garda stations have a **Community Garda**. He or she carries out many of the same tasks a garda does, but has extra responsibilities. One of the main functions of the Community Garda is to get to know people who live and work in the community. Developing links with local businesses, youth workers, sports clubs and other voluntary organisations is an important aspect of their job.

An Garda Síochána try to educate the public about crime prevention and have been involved in crime prevention schemes such as **Neighbourhood Watch** in urban areas and **Community Alert** in rural areas. These schemes encourage communities to become actively involved in preventing and reporting crime in their local areas.

Take action!

Invite the Community Garda to your school to talk to your class about their job and about how you can get involved in crime prevention.

- ⊘ Being Creative
- ⊘ Being Literate
- ⊘ Communicating
- ⊘ Staying Well
- ⊘ Working with Others

Don't forget to complete your reflections in your reflective journal.

Local, national and international courts

Learning outcomes

By the end of this chapter you will know about the roles of local, national and international courts. You will be able to describe why these courts are relevant to citizens.

Key skills you will use in this chapter

- ✓ Being Creative
- ✓ Being Literate
- ✓ Being Numerate
- ✓ Communicating
- ✓ Managing Information and Thinking
- ✓ Managing Myself
- ✓ Staying Well
- ✓ Working with Others

Wellbeing indicators in this chapter

Key words

- Civil law
- Civil action
- Criminal law
- Director of Public Prosecutions
- District Courts
- Circuit Courts
- High Court
- Case law
- Central Criminal Court
- Special Criminal Court
- Court of Appeal
- Supreme Court
- Children's Court
- In camera
- Small Claims Court

- Solicitor
- Barrister
- Judge
- Tipstaff
- Jury
- Stenographer
- Defendant
- Prosecution
- Witness
- Journalists
- Members of the public
- Prison sentence
- European Court of Justice
- International Court of Justice
- International Criminal Court

Irish law

The court system is another way in which the law is enforced in Ireland. As well as enforcing the law, the main function of a court is to ensure that justice is done and that the outcome of any court case is fair and reasonable. In Ireland, courts deal with two main types of law: civil law and criminal law.

 ## Civil law

Civil law is concerned with disagreements between people or between an individual and an organisation. Anybody can take a **civil action** against another person or group. This often relates to areas such as contracts, employment, wills and property disputes.

People may take a case if they have been injured through no fault of their own. There is a separate civil court that deals specifically with family law issues such as custody, divorce and separation.

 ## Criminal law

Criminal law deals with criminal offences such as theft, assault, armed robbery, rape and murder. Unlike civil cases, the state brings a case against a person suspected of a crime. The person responsible for making a case on behalf of the state is the **Director of Public Prosecutions**. It is up to a jury, under the direction of a judge, to decide the facts of a case and conclude whether or not the defendant(s) is guilty of a particular crime.

The court system in Ireland

The main function of a court is to apply the law, to hear both sides and to ensure that fair procedure has been followed. The court system in Ireland is made up of a number of courts, each with a particular responsibility.

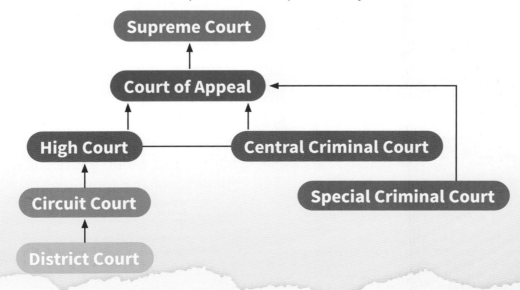

The District Court

The **District Courts** are the busiest in the Irish legal system and hear more cases than any other court. There are twenty-three District Courts throughout Ireland. They deal with minor civil cases such as debt collection, alcohol and lottery licensing and personal injury claims where the compensation is no more than €15,000.

This court also deals with minor criminal cases, such as road traffic and public order offences. The judge weighs up the evidence and decides the outcome of the case. There is no jury in a District Court. If someone is dissatisfied with the judge's decision, they can make an appeal to the Circuit Court.

The Circuit Court

There are eight **Circuit Courts** throughout Ireland. The outcome of cases in the District Court can be appealed to the Circuit Court. This court deals with more serious civil matters and crimes such as armed robbery. A jury decides whether someone is guilty or not guilty of a crime. People who are dissatisfied with the outcome of a court case can appeal to the High Court.

The High Court

The **High Court** hears appeals from the Circuit Court and the most serious civil cases. Depending on the nature of the case, the judge may decide to hold a trial with or without a jury.

Rulings in the High Court are significant because the decisions made there become **case law**. The decisions made in the High Court can be used as a precedent (guide) in court cases in the future.

The Central Criminal Court

When dealing with criminal cases, the High Court is known as the **Central Criminal Court**. It hears the most serious criminal cases, such as rape and murder. In these cases, a jury decides whether the defendant is guilty or not guilty of a crime. If someone is found guilty, the judge determines the sentence.

The Special Criminal Court

The **Special Criminal Court** hears cases related to terrorism and gangland crime. There is no jury present and there are three judges.

The Court of Appeal

The **Court of Appeal** hears appeals from the High Court and the Circuit Court. This court has a president and nine judges.

The Supreme Court

The **Supreme Court** is the highest court in Ireland. The court has five judges and no jury. This court hears appeals from the High Court. In most cases it is not possible to appeal the decision of the Supreme Court unless the decision is in breach of European law.

Sometimes the President may refer a bill to this court to see if it is constitutional. If it is found to be against the constitution, it will not become law.

There are other courts with a special role to play.

The Children's Court

The **Children's Court** deals with cases involving children under the age of eighteen. Children charged with an offence are not allowed to be identified. Therefore, cases in the Children's Court are held **in camera**. This means that the public are not allowed to sit in on cases.

The Small Claims Court

The **Small Claims Court** deals with consumers who have a dispute with a retailer or business. The maximum claim is €2,000.

Take action!

Track a high-profile court case that is currently in the media. Who is involved in the court case and what are the facts of the case? Follow this court case through to its conclusion. Do you agree with the verdict? Why or why not?

- ⊘ Being Creative
- ⊘ Being Literate
- ⊘ Managing Information and Thinking
- ⊘ Managing Myself

The key players in the court system

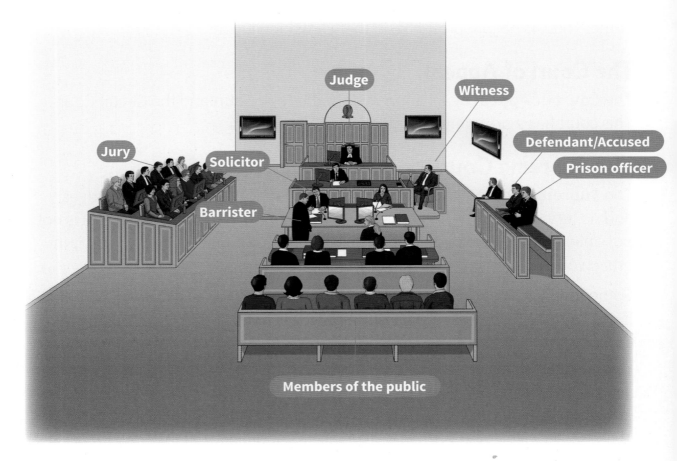

Solicitor

A **solicitor** is usually the first port of call if a person is seeking advice or help with a legal matter. Solicitors advise their clients on both civil and criminal matters. Solicitors deal with a wide range of legal matters, such as family law, property law and criminal law. If a legal matter goes to court, the solicitor prepares the case for court. They appoint a barrister to represent their client in court if necessary, or the solictior can represent the client themselves.

Barrister

When a case goes to court, a **barrister** is employed by a solicitor to speak on behalf of the person involved in the court case. The role of the barrister is to argue the client's case, state the law and question any witnesses.

Judge

Judges are experts in the law. They are in charge during a court case. The judge instructs the jury on legal issues. If a defendant is found guilty, the judge decides the prison sentence if there is one.

Tipstaff

The **tipstaff** is the judge's assistant in court. He or she announces the arrival and departure of the judge in court and asks everyone in the courtroom to stand when the judge enters or leaves.

Jury

The **jury** is made up of twelve people who decide, based on the evidence presented in court, whether a person is innocent or guilty of a crime. Juries are randomly selected from the electoral register.

Stenographer

The **stenographer** is responsible for taking notes and reporting on everything said during a court case. They produce a transcript, which is useful if the case goes to appeal to a higher court.

Defendant

In criminal court cases, a **defendant** is someone who has been accused of a crime. They can also be referred to as 'the accused'. The defendant is often accompanied by a prison officer in court.

Defence and prosecution

In a criminal trial, the **prosecution** is the state. The prosecution's job is to prove that the accused is guilty beyond a reasonable doubt. The role of the defence is to ensure that the defendant receives a fair trial and that the defendant's rights are upheld. A person is innocent until proven guilty.

Witness

A **witness** could be someone who saw a crime being committed or it could be an expert in a subject that is relevant to the case.

Journalists

In high-profile court cases, **journalists** are usually present in the courtroom. They record decisions made by the court. This keeps the public informed.

Members of the public

In most court cases, **members of the public** are allowed to sit in on proceedings. They sit in the public gallery.

Crime and punishment

If someone is found guilty of breaking the law, they must be punished or penalised in some way.

Sometimes people are given a caution. This is a warning that if they end up in court again, they may receive a tougher punishment.

In the case of driving offences, penalty points can be awarded, or the dangerous driver could be sent to a speed awareness course.

Sometimes people will be fined or given community service to do.

Citizens found guilty of serious crimes receive a **prison sentence**.

Debate

- ✓ Being Creative
- ✓ Being Literate
- ✓ Communicating
- ✓ Managing Information and Thinking
- ✓ Managing Myself
- ✓ Working with Others

Organise a debate on the following topic:

💬 'The justice system in Ireland is too lenient on criminals.'

Having completed this debate, has your opinion changed or has it stayed the same? Can you explain why?

European courts

EU member states must obey EU laws. The European Court of Justice was established to enforce these laws.

European Court of Justice

Set up in 1952, the **European Court of Justice** is responsible for making sure that EU laws are upheld. It consists of judges from member states who are appointed to the court for a term of six years. This court is based in Luxembourg.

The main responsibility of this court is to reach decisions in disputes that arise:

🌐 Between member states

🌐 Between the EU and its member states

The European Court of Justice

🌐 Between institutions

🌐 Between private individuals and their state.

International courts

You have learned about International Law and the importance of keeping peace between countries and protecting the rights of citizens worldwide. There are two main courts that defend international law.

The International Court of Justice

The **International Court of Justice** is located in the Hague in the Netherlands. This court was established by the United Nations in 1946. The main function of this court is to settle disagreements between countries and offer advice and opinions on legal matters. Common disputes involve clashes over territory, maritime (sea) boundaries and violations (breaches) of trade agreements.

This court also deals with criminal law and human rights breaches. Fifteen judges sit on this court.

The International Criminal Court

The **International Criminal Court** is an independent permanent court that investigates and tries individuals suspected of crimes against humanity. This court was set up in 2002 and is located in the Hague in the Netherlands.

Thomas Lubanga

The court is made up of eighteen judges who serve a term of nine years. They make sure that the accused receives a fair trial. If a person is found guilty, the court can impose sentences up to life imprisonment and the person found guilty may be required to pay compensation to the victims.

Thomas Lubanga, a militia commander in the Democratic Republic of the Congo, was the first person to be convicted by the International Criminal Court. Lubanga was accused of grave human rights violations. Rebels under his command massacred, raped and tortured civilians. He was also accused of recruiting child soldiers who committed acts of violence and murder. Lubanga was found guilty in 2012 and is now serving a prison sentence.

Take action!

- ⊘ Being Creative
- ⊘ Being Literate
- ⊘ Communicating
- ⊘ Managing Information and Thinking
- ⊘ Managing Myself
- ⊘ Working with Others

Role play

- ❯ Hold a mock trial on the theft of a smartphone in your class.

- ❯ Decide which person plays the role of the accused and what the evidence is against them.

- ❯ Choose someone to play the barrister for the prosecution.

- ❯ Choose someone to play the barrister for the defence.

- ❯ Nominate twelve people to sit on the jury.

- ❯ Nominate one person to play the judge. The judge must decide on the sentence if the defendant is found guilty.

- ❯ Make sure that you have witnesses for the defence and for the prosecution.

Don't forget to complete your reflections in your reflective journal.

How the law helps prevent discrimination

Learning outcomes

By the end of this chapter you will understand the nine grounds under which discrimination is illegal in Ireland.

Key words

⚷ Equal Status Acts
⚷ Employment Equality Acts
⚷ Workplace Relations Commission
⚷ Adjudication officer

Key skills you will use in this chapter

- ✓ Being Creative
- ✓ Being Literate
- ✓ Being Numerate
- ✓ Communicating
- ✓ Managing Information and Thinking
- ✓ Managing Myself
- ✓ Staying Well
- ✓ Working with Others

Wellbeing indicators in this chapter

Discrimination and the law

In Strand 1 you learned about discrimination and the impact it has on its victims. Discrimination occurs when some people are treated less favourably than others. Some suffer harassment and victimisation, which can be direct or indirect.

One of the most important aspects of law is to protect people's rights. Over the years, laws have been introduced to prevent discrimination. Two of the most important legal developments in this area in Ireland are:

1   The Equal Status Acts, 2000–2015

2   The Employment Equality Acts, 1998–2015

The Equal Status Acts, 2000–2015

The **Equal Status Acts** are a series of laws that forbid discrimination in areas such as:

🌐 The provision of goods and services

🌐 Education

🌐 The provision of accommodation services.

The main aim of the Equal Status Acts is to promote equality in Irish society and to prevent discrimination, harassment and victimisation of individuals and groups. The Equal Status Acts prohibit discrimination on the following nine grounds.

Gender

You are entitled to equal treatment if you are female, male or transgender.

Disability

You are entitled to be treated equally if you have a disability, whether it is a physical, intellectual or learning disability. Disability also refers to long-term medical conditions.

Religion

You are entitled to equal treatment regardless of your religious beliefs or lack of them.

Civil status

Civil status refers to whether you are not married, married, separated, divorced, widowed or in a civil partnership. You must be treated equally regardless of your civil status.

⑤ Family status

You are entitled to be treated equally if you are pregnant or if you are the parent of a child or children under the age of eighteen. This also applies to carers who are caring for people with disabilities who are over the age of eighteen.

⑥ Age

If you are eighteen years or over, you are entitled to be treated in the same manner as any other adult.

⑦ Sexual orientation

Regardless of your sexual orientation, you have the right to be treated equally.

⑧ Membership of the Travelling community

You have the right to be treated the same as members of the settled community.

⑨ Race

You are entitled to be treated equally regardless of race, skin colour and ethnicity.

From January 2016, the Equality (Miscellaneous Provisions) Act introduced housing assistance as a new discriminatory ground. This means that people in receipt of a rent supplement, housing assistance payments or social welfare payments may not be discriminated against for that reason. It is illegal for landlords to refuse to accept tenants who receive some form of housing assistance or social welfare from the government.

The Employment Equality Acts, 1998–2015

The **Employment Equality Acts** forbid discrimination in the workplace under the same nine grounds as the Equal Status Acts. These laws also cover work experience and training.

In addition to the nine grounds, these Acts also cover specific situations. These include:

🌐 **Disability:** Employers must make reasonable arrangements for workers with disabilities. This includes access to employment and providing training and promotion opportunities to an employee with a disability.

🌐 **Pregnancy:** This is related to discrimination on the basis of gender. A woman cannot be discriminated against because she is pregnant. Recruitment and promotion should not be denied.

🌐 **Equal pay:** These laws ensure equal pay for equal work. A claim for equal pay can be made on any of the nine grounds.

The Workplace Relations Commission

The **Workplace Relations Commission (WRC)** is an organisation that hears and decides equality cases under the Equal Status Acts and Employment Equality Acts. People can contact the commission if they feel that they have been discriminated against. If their claim is investigated, an **adjudication officer** from the commission assesses evidence and decides if the situation is unlawful.

An Coimisiún um Chaidreamh san Áit Oibre
Workplace Relations Commission

To make a complaint under the Equal Status Acts, you must notify the person or organisation you are making the complaint against, within two months. If they have made no response or you are not happy with their response, you can refer your complaint to the WRC. The WRC will investigate your complaint and may mediate on your behalf if they feel that your rights have been violated.

✓ Being Creative
✓ Being Literate
✓ Communicating
✓ Managing Information and Thinking
✓ Managing Myself
✓ Staying Well
✓ Working with Others

Take action!

Organise a poster campaign in your school to raise awareness about the Equal Status Acts. Your posters should include the nine grounds relating to discrimination.

 Don't forget to complete your reflections in your reflective journal.

How laws can influence change in society

Learning outcomes

By the end of this chapter you will know about some laws that have brought about a change in Irish society. You will also be able to name some individuals and groups who helped to change the law.

Key skills you will use in this chapter

- ✓ Being Creative
- ✓ Being Literate
- ✓ Being Numerate
- ✓ Communicating
- ✓ Managing Information and Thinking
- ✓ Managing Myself
- ✓ Staying Well
- ✓ Working with Others

Key words

- 🔑 Marriage bar
- 🔑 Decriminalise
- 🔑 Protest
- 🔑 Petition
- 🔑 Lobbying

Wellbeing indicators in this chapter

Using the law to bring about change

Laws can help to mould and change our society. Let's look at some important laws that have brought about a positive change in Irish society over the years.

🌐 1908: Old Age Pension Act

🌐 1967: Free secondary education

🌐 1976: Family Law Act

🌐 1977: Employment Equality Act

🌐 1998: Education Welfare Act

🌐 2000–2015: Equal Status Acts

🌐 2000: Minimum Wage Act

🌐 2004: The smoking ban

🌐 2015: Marriage Equality Act

Group activity

✓ Being Creative
✓ Being Literate
✓ Communicating
✓ Managing Information and Thinking
✓ Managing Myself
✓ Staying Well
✓ Working with Others

Divide the class into groups. In your group, choose one of the laws listed above. For that law, discuss the following:

✲ The reasons why you think the law was introduced

✲ The impact that the law has had on Irish citizens.

Write down your thoughts in your copybook and report back to the class.

The status of women and the law

The role and status of women in Irish society has changed dramatically over the past number of decades. Some laws today promote gender equality, but some laws from recent decades did the opposite.

A woman being ejected for interrupting a speech given by Augustine Birrell, Chief Secretary for Ireland in Herbert Asquith's Liberal government

Married women could not hold a job in the civil service

Up until the 1970s, a law prevented married women from holding a job in the civil service, health boards, banks and local authorities. When a woman got married, she had to give up her job. This was known as the **marriage bar**.

Many women's groups in Ireland at that time campaigned against this law and held protests to highlight the discrimination against women. The marriage bar was finally removed in 1973. In 1977 the government introduced the Employment Equality Act, which prohibited discrimination in the workplace on the grounds of gender or marital status.

Women could not sit on a jury

Under the 1927 Juries Act, to sit on a jury in Ireland you had to be a property owner. At that time in Ireland most property owners were men, so in effect this law prevented women from doing jury duty.

In 1976, two women's rights campaigners, Máirín de Burca and Mary Anderson, challenged this law in the Supreme Court. They won their case and the old Act was repealed. Thanks to the actions of these women, any person over the age of eighteen on the electoral register is eligible to sit on a jury.

Máirín de Burca

Women's rights in public houses

In the past, public houses treated women differently from men. There were no laws to prevent this treatment. Some pubs did not allow women on their premises. Other pubs allowed women as long as they were accompanied by a man. In some cases, women were not allowed to buy or drink a pint of beer in a pub.

Many women's groups highlighted this inequality. One campaigner, Nell McCafferty, brought a group of women into a pub and they ordered and were served thirty brandies. When they ordered a pint of stout, the barman refused to serve them. The women drank their brandies but refused to pay because their order had not been served. The actions of these women highlighted gender inequality in Irish society. Gender inequality was finally addressed with the introduction of the Equal Status Acts.

Nell McCafferty

Individuals who have changed the law

There are other individuals and groups whose actions have brought about a change in the law.

Kathy Sinnott is a disability rights campaigner. In 2000 she took a court case to force the government to provide primary education for her son, who had multiple

disabilities. In 2001 the High Court ruled that every child under the age of eighteen had a constitutional right to a primary education based on need.

For many years, Irish law said that sexual acts between two men were a crime. David Norris, a senator in Seanad Éireann, brought cases before the High Court and the Supreme Court to challenge the criminalisation of homosexuality. However, the courts ruled against him. David Norris then brought his case to the European Court of Human Rights. This court ruled that this Irish law went against the Convention on Human Rights. As a result, the law changed in Ireland. In 1993, a new law was introduced that **decriminalised** homosexuality.

David Norris

Groups that have changed the law

There have also been groups that have challenged the law or have brought about a change in the law in Irish society.

The Right2Water campaign

When the Irish government passed a law to introduce water charges, many people were unhappy. The Right2Water campaign held protests, a social media campaign and a poster campaign that succeeded in the water charges being suspended (delayed).

The marriage equality campaign

In 2015, the government held a referendum on marriage equality rights. This referendum asked the Irish people if they agreed with changing the constitution to allow same–sex marriage. To win support for a Yes vote, the Yes for Equality campaign was set up. This campaign was very successful and the Yes vote got nearly 63% of the votes. This was an important milestone not only in Irish law, but internationally.

Can I influence the law?

Living in a democracy means that you have the right to challenge the government. You also have the right to challenge the law if you think it is unfair or if it takes away your human rights.

There are many ways in which you can influence the law and highlight the need for a change in the law. These include the following.

Protests

Many groups that want to change the law organise **protests**. Protests help to highlight issues and make the public aware of why the law needs to change. Many groups and organisations use posters and social media platforms to gain support for their cause.

Organising a petition

Organising a **petition** involves collecting signatures. This petition is usually given to a member of government to show that many people are in favour of this change.

Lobbying politicians or government ministers

Lobbying involves putting pressure on politicians or members of government. You can lobby a politician to bring about a change in the law. Lobbying can involve letter-writing campaigns, emails, phone calls and meetings.

Challenging the law in court

If you think that the law is unfair and violates (doesn't respect) your rights under the Irish constitution, you can bring your case to court.

 Take action!

- ⊘ Being Creative
- ⊘ Being Literate
- ⊘ Communicating
- ⊘ Managing Information and Thinking
- ⊘ Managing Myself
- ⊘ Staying Well
- ⊘ Working with Others

Think about a law that you believe is unfair or needs to be changed. Describe an action that you could undertake to highlight the need to change this law.

 Don't forget to complete your reflections in your reflective journal.

Mass media

Learning outcomes

By the end of this chapter you will have explored the role of different types of media in generating information and news, and you will have assessed the pros and cons of each type.

Key skills you will use in this chapter

- ✓ Being Creative
- ✓ Being Literate
- ✓ Being Numerate
- ✓ Communicating
- ✓ Managing Information and Thinking
- ✓ Managing Myself
- ✓ Staying Well
- ✓ Working with Others

Key words

- Mass media
- State agencies
- Constitution
- Freedom of expression
- Freedom of Information Act
- Bias
- Fake news
- Clickbait
- Traditional media
- Mainstream media
- New media
- Digital media
- Social media
- Cyberbullying
- Digital generation
- Digital citizen

Wellbeing indicators in this chapter

What is media?

Media is the plural of the word *medium*. We use the phrase **mass media** to describe the means of communication, including radio, television, newspapers, magazines and the internet, that reach or influence people widely.

Mass media helps to spread information to large numbers of people. It keeps people connected with events locally, nationally and internationally.

The twentieth century saw a growth in the types of media used. At the beginning of that century, traditional types of media were word of mouth, newspaper and radio. However, by the end of the century and into this century, mass media has changed dramatically.

A wide range of television channels, internet sites and other types of media have meant that more and more information is being made available to people. This is happening at a very fast pace.

Freedom of the media

In most democratic societies, freedom of the media is a right. This means that the media can report on, communicate and express opinions in a variety of ways.

Freedom of the media means that there is no interference from government or other **state agencies**. Many countries have made sure that this freedom is guaranteed by writing it into the **constitution** of the country. Article 19 of the Universal Declaration of Human Rights also promotes the right to **freedom of expression**. This means that everyone, including people in the media, has a right to express their opinions without fear.

? Questions

Freedom of the media (press) varies from country to country.

⊘ Being Literate
⊘ Managing Information and Thinking
⊘ Managing Myself

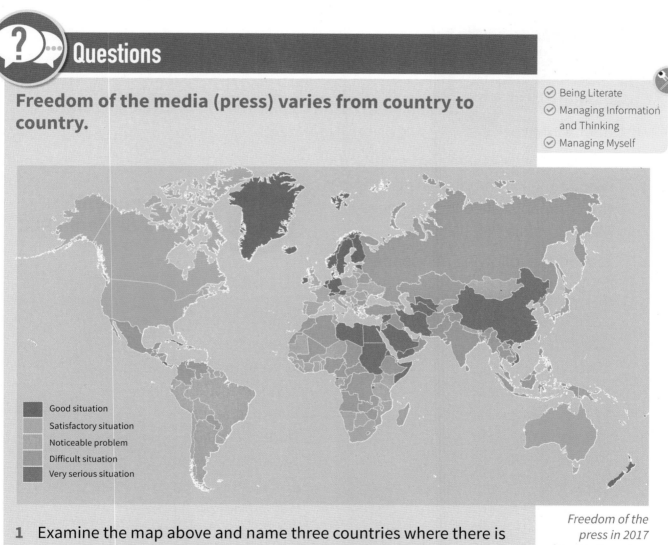

- Good situation
- Satisfactory situation
- Noticeable problem
- Difficult situation
- Very serious situation

Freedom of the press in 2017 (source: Reporters without Borders)

1 Examine the map above and name three countries where there is very limited freedom of the press. Use an atlas to help you.

2 Can you think of one reason why this might be so with one of the countries? Explain your answer.

Freedom of Information Act

In Ireland, we have the **Freedom of Information Act** (FOI). It ensures freedom of the media and access to information. It is particularly important that information stored by government agencies and other official state groups is made available. It means that we can hold these groups accountable. If information is being kept from the public, it will eventually be found out.

Who owns the media?

Most newspapers, magazines and radio stations are owned by companies. Some television stations are owned by private companies. They depend on advertising to make a profit. RTÉ is owned by the state and its income comes from both advertising and the television licence fee.

In Ireland, some large companies own numerous media. One example is a company called Independent News & Media PLC (INM PLC).

It owns the following newspapers:

National newspapers:	Regional newspapers:
Belfast Telegraph	Bray People
Irish Daily Star	Drogheda Independent
Irish Independent	Enniscorthy Guardian
Sunday Independent	Fingal Independent
Sunday Life	Gorey Guardian
Sunday World	New Ross Standard
The Herald	The Argus
	The Corkman
	The Sligo Champion
	Wexford People
	Wicklow People

Another example is a company called Communicorp. It owns Ireland's largest commercial news radio stations, Newstalk and Today FM. The company also owns a number of other radio stations, including Spin 1038 and 98 FM.

The Irish Times is another large media company in Ireland. As well as owning the *Irish Times* newspaper, in 2017 it acquired Landmark Media, a group that owns the *Irish Examiner* and many regional newspapers, including the *Evening Echo*, the *Kildare Nationalist* and the *Roscommon Echo*. Landmark Media also has interests in several radio stations, including WLR RM and Beat 102–103 FM.

News Corp is an international media company. It was founded in Australia in 1979 by Rupert Murdoch but now has its headquarters in New York. It owns television stations, newspapers, film companies, book companies and other types of media. It is a multibillion-dollar company based in more than 100 countries.

Responsibility of the media

One of the media's most important responsibilities is to report on news in a fair way that does not show **bias** (bias is when only one side of a story or argument is told or where one side of the story or argument gets more attention).

If the media are biased, then we don't receive the full story or maybe get only one side of the story. In situations like this, the media can control the information we receive and maybe even control what we think and the opinions we have.

Examples of how the media can be biased

🌐 Deliberately leaving out an important piece of information in a story

🌐 Relying on information from someone who is not reliable

🌐 Using a headline that focuses on one side of the story.

Fake news

During the US presidential campaign in 2016, the term '**fake news**' became popular. Some people believe it was part of the reason why Donald Trump got elected. Many people now agree that Trump used fake news to promote his policies and opinions.

Fake news means that the story is completely made up and not based on fact. It is used to mislead people and is probably more widespread than we realise. We should examine news stories carefully and in detail. Media is a profit-driven industry and some media companies may spread fake news to increase audience numbers or readership.

Clickbait

Media companies have been known to use **clickbait** to attract an audience or readers. This is where they use deliberately misleading or sensationalist headlines. Not all clickbait leads to fake news, but fake news will often use clickbait to attract attention.

💡 Imagine!

☑ Being Creative
☑ Being Literate
☑ Communicating
☑ Managing Information and Thinking
☑ Managing Myself
☑ Working with Others

Imagine that you have been asked to write a newspaper article for your local newspaper. Your article will be on the front page and must attract as many readers as possible.

Design an article based on fake news with an appropriate clickbait headline.

Debate

☑ Being Creative
☑ Being Literate
☑ Communicating
☑ Managing Information and Thinking
☑ Managing Myself
☑ Working with Others

Organise a walking debate on one of the following topics:

- 'People's opinions are controlled by media companies.'
- 'Freedom of the media is impossible.'

Having completed this debate, has your opinion changed or stayed the same? Can you explain why?

Mainstream media and new media

It is now common to call **traditional media** such as newspapers, television news and radio **mainstream media**, while newer types of media available online are referred to as **new media**. New media can be created and viewed on devices such as computers, tablets, smartphones and via satellite television. New media can be interactive (we can read, listen and watch, but now we can also comment and report on these). The term **digital media** is also used to refer to these interactive types of media.

As soon as something happens in most parts of the world today, it is almost immediately reported on by an organisation or by ordinary people using tablets or smartphones. It is now possible for anybody to create content and display it for the world to see.

These and many other media platforms are easily accessible in a democratic society. You probably access some of these regularly.

The rise of digital media

Most traditional types of media companies now offer both traditional and digital media. For example, the majority of Irish newspapers have both a printed edition and a digital version.

Many experts believe that traditional print media (newspapers and magazines) are in decline and will soon be replaced by digital forms of media. They believe that young people, like you, prefer to access information via digital sources rather than traditional ones, such as print.

Traditional and digital media companies make money from advertising. Look at your local or national newspaper and you will see many advertisements. Without the money received from these, newspapers and magazines would not be able to exist. The rise of digital media means that companies are investing more and more money in advertising on digital media.

Think, pair and share

- ⊘ Being Creative
- ⊘ Being Literate
- ⊘ Communicating
- ⊘ Managing Information and Thinking
- ⊘ Managing Myself
- ⊘ Working with Others

Think about the terms *mainstream media* and *new media*. With your partner:

1 Draw up a list of mainstream media sources and new media sources. Write the list in your copybook.

2 Explain why people might use a variety of media sources and what the difference is between them. When you have completed your list, report back to your class.

Use the table in your reflective journal to write down your ideas.

Social media

In the activity above, you probably included some examples of new media called **social media**. Social media is probably the most popular form of new media, particularly among young people. Social media refers to any platform that is used by large numbers of people to interact with one another. You might use one or more of these on a regular basis to communicate with friends, family and strangers. Facebook, Instagram, TikTok and Twitter are some of the most popular social media platforms used today.

 Video Think before you share

Like all forms of media, social media has positive and negative aspects. Here is a list of some of the pros and cons of social media for young people.

Positive	Negative
You can meet new people and make new friends.	Adults can make up false information and stalk and lure children online.
You can keep in touch with friends and family who are not nearby.	Some young people can post too much personal information, such as addresses and telephone numbers.
You can share news and post photographs and videos to friends.	You can waste lots of time and become addicted to some platforms. You can forget to make eye contact with people and look around you to experience the real world.
You can join groups that share your interests by chatting and discussing.	It is easy to say negative things or to bully other young people on these platforms. This is referred to as cyberbullying.
	You can suffer from 'putting your best face forward' syndrome or being 'on' for the camera. Life is messy, but online profiles can give the impression that everyone else's life is perfect.

Cyberbullying

Unfortunately, one major problem associated with the use of social media is **cyberbullying**. This happens when people use digital technology such as tablets and smartphones to bully others. Examples of cyberbullying include:

- Sending mean texts or emails
- Spreading rumours on social media sites
- Posting embarrassing photos or videos
- Creating fake profiles.

There have been many tragic stories of young people who have been cyberbullied. One such case was that of Phoebe Prince.

Phoebe was a fifteen-year-old girl from Ireland who moved to Massachusetts in the US. From the moment she attended her new school, she was tormented and bullied by a group of students. She was bullied at school by this group and even when she went home, the bullying continued. The bullies used social network sites including Facebook and Twitter to make Phoebe's life a misery. They sent her threatening posts and text messages calling her incredibly horrible names. She didn't know where to turn for help. The abuse got so intense that Phoebe took her own life.

- ✓ Being Literate
- ✓ Communicating
- ✓ Managing Information and Thinking
- ✓ Managing Myself
- ✓ Staying Well

Research

For more information on cyberbullying, visit the Stop Cyberbullying website.

How to be a good digital citizen

You have learned about the importance of playing an active role in a democracy. Since you are part of the **digital generation**, you should also be aware of your responsibilities to be a good **digital citizen**. The following are some useful tips on how to be a good digital citizen.

1 Don't believe all the information you see on the internet.

2 Be nice to people online.

3 Stay safe online. Don't give out personal information.

4 Think very carefully before sharing a photograph or video online.

5 Be careful not to break laws when online. For example, don't download illegal files.

6 Report and record bad online behaviour.

7 Some people deliberately try to hurt other people with comments. They are known as trolls. They rely on you reacting to their comments. Ignore them.

8 Don't create a false identity online.

9 Remember, some people pretend to be someone they are not. Always be wary of strangers online.

Take action!

Create a short video clip to provide some practical tips for fellow students on how they can help to prevent cyberbullying. Your finished video could be used as a resource for your school's Wellbeing programme.

⊘ Being Creative
⊘ Being Literate
⊘ Communicating
⊘ Managing Information and Thinking
⊘ Managing Myself
⊘ Staying Well
⊘ Working with Others

Don't forget to complete your reflections in your reflective journal.

Chapter 34

The impact of digital media: A case study

Learning outcomes

By the end of this chapter you will understand the term *digital media*. You will be able to refer to examples of digital media. You will also understand how digital media influenced a high-profile election.

Key words

- Candidates
- Millennial generation
- Campaign team

Key skills you will use in this chapter

- ✓ Being Creative
- ✓ Being Literate
- ✓ Being Numerate
- ✓ Communicating
- ✓ Managing Information and Thinking
- ✓ Managing Myself
- ✓ Staying Well
- ✓ Working with Others

Wellbeing indicators in this chapter

The impact digital media can have

The 2016 presidential election in the United States was the most reported-upon campaign in the history of presidential elections. People from all over the world were able to follow the campaign every day. The use of digital media by all the **candidates** (people who put themselves forward for election) made information easily available to everyone.

Case study

It was the use of social media by the two main candidates – Hillary Clinton and Donald Trump – that made information widely accessible. Hillary Clinton first announced on Snapchat that she would be running for President.

Some reports suggest that spending on digital media during the campaign cost approximately $1 billion. Half of that money was spent on social media campaigns.

 Imagine!

Imagine that you were the campaign manager for one of the defeated candidates in the 2016 US presidential election.

1 In your copybook, write a list of social media platforms that you would like to use to promote your candidate for the next presidential election.

2 Explain why you would use each of these platforms to promote your candidate.

- ✓ Being Creative
- ✓ Being Literate
- ✓ Communicating
- ✓ Managing Information and Thinking
- ✓ Managing Myself
- ✓ Working with Others

How 'real' was the social media campaign?

Critics of these social media campaigns argue that too much of the news associated with them was fake news and was used to mislead voters. However, others claim that social media made the candidates accessible to people. For example, Hillary Clinton and Donald Trump frequently used Twitter to make announcements and sometimes criticise the other candidate.

Advertising on digital media during the campaign

Both of the main candidates, Clinton and Trump, realised the importance of advertising on all forms of digital media. Trump's **campaign team** (the group of people who decide on the best way to promote their candidate) really pushed advertising on social media. Despite this focus, Clinton received the majority of young people's votes.

The Trump campaign knew how important it was to keep Trump's profile high on social media through advertising. In fact, it didn't even matter whether what was being said online was true or not as long as it was promoting Donald Trump's name and personality.

Research

- ⊘ Being Creative
- ⊘ Being Literate
- ⊘ Being Numerate
- ⊘ Communicating
- ⊘ Managing Information and Thinking
- ⊘ Managing Myself
- ⊘ Working with Others

Go online to research the impact social media had on the outcome of the 2016 US presidential election.

In your research, identify the type of information that was made available to voters.

1 How important was fake news in deciding the outcome?

2 How did advertising play a role in the outcome?

3 What percentage of the **millennial generation** voted and who did they vote for?

 ## Take action!

- ⊘ Being Creative
- ⊘ Being Literate
- ⊘ Managing Information and Thinking
- ⊘ Managing Myself
- ⊘ Staying Well
- ⊘ Working with Others

Organise an awareness-raising campaign highlighting the uses of digital media in a recent election or referendum. You could present your findings in a digital format.

 Don't forget to complete your reflections in your reflective journal.

Sample citizenship action: A mock election

During our study of Strand 3: Exploring Democracy, the Taoiseach announced that he was dissolving parliament and calling a general election. We had recently learned about the voting process in our CSPE class, and in consultation with our teacher we decided to hold a mock general election of our own. The election would mirror the election in our local constituency and all Third Year students in the school would be eligible to vote.

We were organised into seven different committees. Each committee had a specific responsibility and each member of each committee had a specific role to play. The following are the committees and their responsibilities.

- **Register of electors committee:** This committee had to collect the names and details of all Third Year students. The names of all the students were put on a list in alphabetical order and this became our register of electors.

- **Advertising committee:** This committee made posters to advertise the upcoming election. The members made posters and flyers for the candidates. They also put information about the time, date and other arrangements for the election on the school website and the school announcements page.

- **Polling card committee:** This committee designed a polling card based on a real polling card. The members copied and printed the required number of cards for everyone on the register of electors. They also made sure that everyone on the register received their polling card in time for the election.

- **Ballot paper committee:** This committee designed a ballot paper with all the names of the candidates from our constituency. The members made sure that these were put in alphabetical order. They then photocopied the exact number needed for the mock election.

- **Ballot box committee:** This committee had to source a ballot box for the election. A large box was covered in black paper. One of the members cut out an opening in the box for ballot papers to be placed inside. The members of this committee were responsible for the security of the box and the completed ballot papers during the course of the mock election.

- **Presiding officers committee:** This committee had overall responsibility for running the election on the day. The members had to set up the polling station in the school hall. They enlisted the help of the school caretaker to set up a screen so that students could complete the ballot in secrecy. This committee also had responsibility for checking the names off the register and making sure that nobody voted more than once.

> **The count committee:** This committee was responsible for counting votes. Using the PR system, the members decided who was to be eliminated after each count and eventually worked out the candidates who were deemed elected.

The mock election was a great success. It really helped us to understand how voting works. We hope that it will encourage students to become more active in the democratic process.

Strand 3: Suggested actions

Now take action to enhance your learning.

The following are suggested actions that are linked mainly to Strand 3.

Imagine you are running for election. Make a badge and an election poster designed to inform potential voters about your priorities and proposals.

Conduct a survey to find out what students think about the decision-making processes in your school and how these might be improved. Share your findings.

Participate in an election count using the PR system. Compare the PR system with one other system of voting.

Organise a mock election/referendum in parallel with an election/referendum in real time. Compare the results.

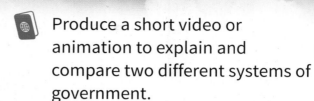

 Produce a short video or animation to explain and compare two different systems of government.

 Participate in a debate on the following motion: 'Young people don't need the vote to have power and influence in our world today.'

 Design a game or infographic to help your peers understand the workings of the Equality Tribunal, European Court of Human Rights or the International Criminal Court.

 Use or create images (no words) to show the nine grounds under which discrimination is illegal in Ireland.

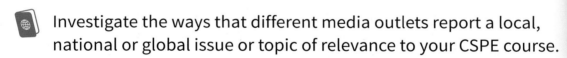 Investigate the ways that different media outlets report a local, national or global issue or topic of relevance to your CSPE course.

 Create a 'how to' guide for people who want to be active online citizens. Include a glossary of key terms, profiles of relevant social media platforms, and case studies of individuals or groups who have used these platforms to bring about positive change in our world.

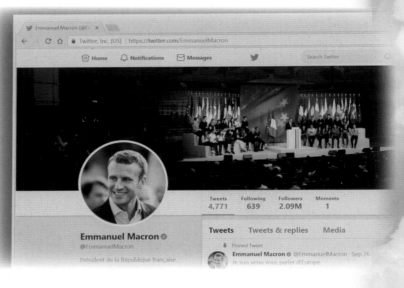

 Investigate the use of social media by one or more politicians.

Chapter 35

Taking action, recording, reflecting and assessment

There are suggestions and opportunities for taking action throughout this book. Taking action is a very important part of CSPE. It helps you to develop skills and gather more information on a particular topic or issue. It should be an enjoyable experience and your teacher will guide you through the process.

You are required to undertake three actions over the duration of the CSPE short course, one action on each of the three strands:

1 Rights and responsibilities

2 Global citizenship

3 Exploring democracy.

Taking action

There are a number of steps that you and your classmates can follow to take action.

Taking Action

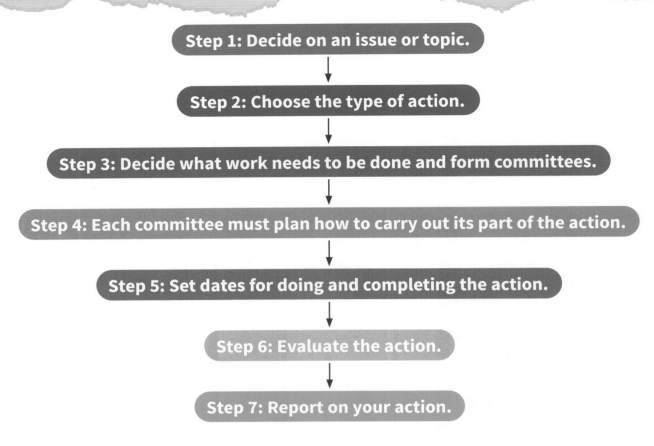

Step 1: Decide on an issue or topic.

↓

Step 2: Choose the type of action.

↓

Step 3: Decide what work needs to be done and form committees.

↓

Step 4: Each committee must plan how to carry out its part of the action.

↓

Step 5: Set dates for doing and completing the action.

↓

Step 6: Evaluate the action.

↓

Step 7: Report on your action.

Step 1

Decide on an issue or topic from the strand you are studying. The issue or topic may have been suggested already in this textbook. If any of the suggestions did not interest you or your classmates, then your teacher could spend part of a class lesson brainstorming to come up with a suggestion.

Step 2

Choose the type of action that you and your classmates want to do to achieve this. There are many ways in which you can take action. By doing so, you are becoming an active citizen and an active learner.

The following are some ways to take action:

- 🌐 Organise a poster campaign
- 🌐 Sign a petition
- 🌐 Raise awareness about the topic or issue
- 🌐 Write a letter to your local TD, MEP or the relevant minister
- 🌐 Write a letter to a newspaper
- 🌐 Produce an information booklet
- 🌐 Organise a local meeting with a relevant guest speaker
- 🌐 Publish your message on your school website
- 🌐 Create your own digital survey
- 🌐 Get a slot on your local radio
- 🌐 Organise a fundraising campaign
- 🌐 Hold a designated day in your school, e.g. Green-Schools Day
- 🌐 Hold a mock election.

As you already know, it is not always easy to get all your classmates to agree on issues. Therefore, your teacher may have to hold a class vote to decide on the type of action you will take. Once this has been agreed, it is time to move on to the next step.

Step 3

Decide what work needs to be done over the course of the action. The best way to divide up the workload is to set up committees (small groups). Each committee takes responsibility for one piece of work. The members will need to report back to the class on a regular basis.

Step 4

Once everybody has been assigned to a committee, each committee must then plan how to carry out its part of the action. Each person in the group must have a task to do. Each person should record the work done and the skills they used to do the work.

Step 5

Set dates for doing and completing the action. Then go ahead and do the action!

Step 6

Evaluate the action. This is a crucial stage of the action. Decide what went well and what didn't go so well. This is a great way for you, your classmates and your teacher to reflect on the action. You may come up with suggestions for how you would improve the action if you were to do it again.

Self-reflection   Group reflection

Step 7

Report on your action. There are many ways you can do this. You can choose to:

- 🌐 Produce a video
- 🌐 Write a blog
- 🌐 Give an oral presentation
- 🌐 Have a poster presentation
- 🌐 Create a podcast
- 🌐 Publish a report in a newspaper or school newsletter
- 🌐 Write a report for your class or year group.

How to organise yourself during the action

🌐 Keep a record of your work, including any new information you received, anything new that you learned and any resources that you used.

🌐 Use an online tool, e.g. Padlet, to keep all of these organised. Online tools can be used by the committee and the class group to keep a record of all the work. Online tools are also a great way to record and share photos and other digital images.

🌐 Record all your thoughts on the topic or issue.

🌐 Keep a committee diary to ensure that you know key dates for all the committee members.

🌐 Record all the skills that you used during the course of the action.

Recording and reflecting on the action

It is critical that you keep a record of all the things that you do during the course of the action. Reflecting on the action is also an important part of self-assessment.

Your reflective journal has templates that you can use to help record and reflect on your thoughts and skills, the resources you accessed and the materials you collected.

Self-assessment and peer assessment

Self-assessment

By reflecting on what you did and the skills you used, you are becoming an active learner. You will be able to judge your own work and ask for help in areas that you don't understand yet. Others, including your teacher, will then be able to make some suggestions as to how you could improve your work. You could then explain your work to someone else to show how well you understand the topic or issue on which you took action. This is called self-assessment. Self-assessment will be a helpful tool when you prepare to write a Citizenship Action Record in Second or Third Year.

How to self-assess when taking action

Work through steps 1 to 3.

1 Check my understanding

I understand this issue/topic because ...

This main idea is ...

The bit I don't understand is ...

I need to ask my teacher about ...

2 What went well?

The things that went well were ...

I am good at ...

I am proud of ...

My best work is ...

3 How could I improve?

To improve my work I need to ...

To improve the quality of my work, I should ...

Next time I take action, I must remember ...

Peer assessment

You and members of your committee, and indeed your class group, should also take time to look at one another's work. This is **peer assessment**. When you report back to a fellow student on their work, this is called giving feedback. You can learn a lot from looking at how other people organise and present their work, while others can learn from how you organise and present your work. This is a great opportunity to get a better understanding of the topic or issue on which you are taking action.

The best part of your work is...

How to give advice to another student

1 Give the other student feedback, e.g. 'Here are some thoughts I have on your work ...'

2 Give a short comment on what you thought was really good, e.g. 'The best part of your work is ... because ...'

3 Give a short comment on what the student could improve, e.g. 'The part you could improve is ... because ...'

Citizenship Action Record

The last step is to put together a structured report on one of your actions. This is called a Citizenship Action Record. Your Citizenship Action Record will be used as your classroom-based assessment (CBA).

The Citizenship Action Record shows how you have actively engaged in the topic or issue. It requires you to do two key things:

1 Report on the action you undertook.

2 Give your reflections on the experience.

Use the Citizenship Action Record template in your reflective journal to help you.

How to present your Citizenship Action Record

You can present your Citizenship Action Record in one of the following ways:

- 🌐 Written presentation
- 🌐 Digital presentation
- 🌐 Visual presentation
- 🌐 Audio presentation
- 🌐 Visual and audio presentation.

For example, your record can be handwritten, an oral presentation, a video, a digital presentation, a poster presentation or a mix of these. When your Citizenship Action Record has been created, you might get a chance to present some aspects of it, or indeed all of it, to a suitable audience.

Notes

Notes

Notes

Notes